Response to Intervention: An Action Guide for School Leaders

Barbara J. Ehren
Tom C. Ehren
Janet L. Proly

Foreword by Donald D. Deshler, University of Kansas

Because research and information make the difference.

Educational Research Service
1001 North Fairfax Street, Suite 500 • Alexandria, VA 22314
Phone: 703-243-2100 • Toll Free: 800-791-9308
Fax: 703-243-1985 • Toll Free: 800-791-9309
Email: ers@ers.org • Web site: www.ers.org

Because research and information make the difference.

Educational Research Service

1001 North Fairfax Street, Suite 500 • Alexandria, VA 22314-1587
Phone: 703-243-2100 • Toll Free: 800-791-9308
Fax: 703-243-1985 • Toll Free: 800-791-9309
Email: ers@ers.org • Web site: www.ers.org

Educational Research Service is the nonprofit organization providing school leaders with essential research for effective decisions. Founded by the national school management associations, ERS is the school leader's best source for resources and data to build more successful schools. Since 1973, education leaders have utilized the ERS advantage to make the most effective school decisions in both day-to-day operations and long-range planning. Visit us online at www.ers.org for a more complete picture of the wealth of preK-12 research information and tools available through ERS subscriptions and resources.

ERS Founding Organizations:
American Association of School Administrators
American Association of School Personnel Administrators
Association of School Business Officials International
National Association of Elementary School Principals
National Association of Secondary School Principals
National School Public Relations Association

ERS Executive Staff:
John C. Draper, Ed.D., Chief Executive Officer
Katherine A. Behrens, Chief Operating Officer
Kathleen McLane, Chief Knowledge Officer

Library of Congress Cataloging-in-Publication Data
Response to intervention : an action guide for school leaders / by Barbara J. Ehren, Tom C. Ehren, Janet L. Proly ; foreword by Donald Deshler.
    p. cm.
Includes bibliographical references and index.
ISBN 978-1-931762-84-7
      1. Remedial teaching. 2. Reading--Remedial teaching 3. Learning disabled children--Identification. 4. Learning disabilities--Diagnosis. 5. School management and organization. I. Ehren, Tom C. II. Proly, Janet L. III. Title.

LB1029.R4E4 2009
371.43--dc22   2008054646

Authors: Barbara J. Ehren, Tom C. Ehren, and Janet L. Proly
Editors: Kathleen McLane and Cheryl Bratten
Layout & Design: Susie McKinley and Libby McNulty

Ordering Information: Additional copies of *Response to Intervention: An Action Guide for School Leaders* may be purchased at the list price of $30.00; ERS School District Subscriber price: $15; ERS Individual Subscriber price: $22.50. Add the greater of $4.50 or 10% of the total purchase price for shipping and handling. Stock No. 0755. ISBN: 978-1-931762-84-7. Phone orders accepted with Visa, MasterCard, or American Express. Call ERS to order at 800-791-9308 or on the web at www.ers.org.

Note: ERS is solely responsible for this publication; no approval or endorsement by ERS founders is implied.

Table of Contents

Foreword

One of the most significant developments in educational practice during the past decade has been the degree to which Response to Intervention (RTI) has gained traction as a framework for guiding school improvement efforts. Increasingly, state and local educational agencies are using RTI as a means of conceptualizing and measuring effective instruction for *all* students. While there is a growing list of resources available to frontline practitioners to assist them in implementing RTI, none of these resources focuses entirely on the role of the school principal and other building level leaders. Given that successful implementation of RTI is directly dependent on the vision, knowledge, and leadership skill of principals, it is imperative that they be armed with powerful tools to succeed in this challenging assignment. This book provides school leaders with a resource that they will find to be invaluable in providing an understanding of critical RTI concepts and step-by-step guidelines in how to successfully implement an RTI framework in their schools.

Response to Intervention: An Action Guide for School Leaders is in a class of its own. Not only do Dr. Barbara Ehren and her coauthors make a compelling case for RTI as a school reform framework, but they do so in a way that other books do not. The vast majority of books on RTI are somewhat singular in focus. That is, they primarily address specific strategies for operationalizing each tier of an RTI framework, or they emphasize the legislative underpinnings of the emergence of RTI, or they detail how RTI can be used as one component of a learning disabilities determination process; however, they do not address all of these important areas of inquiry in a comprehensive, integrated manner. Not only do Dr. Ehren and her coauthors address each of these areas, but they have accomplished four things that other books on RTI have not. First, the book explains how RTI frameworks can and should leverage existing practices within schools—RTI is not described as an initiative that ignores or minimizes previously successful work by a school staff. Rather, Dr. Ehren and her coauthors describe how successful initiatives should be built upon and enhanced. Second, this book elegantly integrates information about RTI from a variety of perspectives to help the reader appreciate the complexity of the challenge of implementing RTI and the importance of considering varying perspectives. Third, each chapter uses a series of scenarios situated in an elementary, middle, and high school setting to contextualize the key constructs covered in the chapter. These scenarios ground and enhance the readers' understanding of the critical concepts being addressed. Finally, the vital role of change and sustainability is addressed in a very informed and insightful manner. The topics of change and sustainability of innovations should be a part of every book written about RTI, because its successful implementation requires major changes in beliefs, attitudes, roles, and practices by all professionals on a school staff. By tackling this topic head-on, this book correctly acknowledges that RTI is, at its core, a school reform model. Successful reform does not occur without a sophisticated understanding of the change process.

Throughout this book Dr. Ehren demonstrates her remarkable breadth of knowledge about critical learner characteristics, intervention variables, policy levers and the interactions among these factors. She and her coauthors have done a brilliant job of describing the context within which programming solutions must be generated and the form that these solutions must take in order to be embraced by those charged with implementing educational initiatives to improve outcomes significantly.

The organizational framework used in this book is very innovative. It is perfectly suited to school leaders who carry exceedingly heavy loads and responsibilities. It provides hands-on tools, meaningful guiding questions, and valuable reflection activities—all of which will enable school leaders to immediately transfer the information in each chapter into action. One of the most distinguishing attributes of this book is its crisp, concise style. Dr. Ehren and her coauthors have identified the essential information that is needed for school leaders to successfully implement RTI and presented it in a very lucid, user-friendly manner. This book is an extraordinary resource because of Dr. Ehren's extensive experience as a practitioner, scholar, program developer, researcher, and writer. She has a deep understanding of the complexities of school environments, the needs of academically diverse learners, and the dynamics that exist between them.

I believe that this book will provide practitioners with the foundation that they will need to successfully create the kinds of environments and cultures of learning that will promote the successful implementation of an RTI framework. This very readable book is written with passion, vivid examples, and numerous practical suggestions that can be readily implemented. It will become a major resource in advancing our field's understanding and implementation of RTI.

Donald D. Deshler
University of Kansas
Director, Center for Research on Learning
Gene A. Budig Professor of Special Education

About the Authors

Barbara J. Ehren, Ed.D., is a Professor at the University of Central Florida and Director of a doctoral program which focuses on language and literacy for struggling learners. Previously she was a research scientist with the University of Kansas Center for Research on Learning (KUCRL) where her emphasis was on strategic reading for adolescents, collaboration among professionals in schools, and school-wide literacy initiatives in secondary schools, including Response to Intervention (RTI). Her experience includes many years in public schools as a speech-language pathologist, teacher, and district administrator. She serves on many committees and editorial boards, including the Advisory Board of the RTI Action Network and the International Reading Association Commission on RTI. She has a special interest in assisting school systems to build capacity at the school level for more effective literacy programs for diverse learners. She is a frequent consultant to states, school districts, and professional associations on RTI-related issues.

Tom C. Ehren, M.S., is a Clinical Instructor at the University of Central Florida. Prior to this position he worked for over 30 years in Florida school districts, most of them as a district administrator. Special projects included work at the building level to enhance literacy achievement and collaboration with families. He has been an invited speaker to many educational agencies, and state and national associations on literacy leadership, including Response to Intervention. His professional interests include program design, school-level literacy initiatives, innovative professional development, advocacy, and leadership development.

Janet L. Proly, M.A., is a full-time doctoral student at the University of Central Florida, focusing on language and literacy in children and adolescents. She has a special interest in systems change in the schools, especially Response to Intervention. Her experience as an educator in pubic schools includes working as a speech-language pathologist in middle school. She has a B.A. in Communications with a specialty in Advertising/Public Relations and several years of experience in advertising sales. Her diverse experiences have given her a broad perspective on dealing effectively with a variety of populations.

Prologue

It is now commonplace to hear Response to Intervention (RTI) discussed in educational circles and to read about it in professional publications. However, as the word gets out, there seems to be growing confusion over what it actually is. Is it a special education initiative? Is it meant only for elementary schools? Do schools have to do it? Is literacy the required focus? How is it different from the reform efforts already underway in our district? Do I have to abandon other initiatives at my school in order to adopt RTI? These are a few of the questions school leaders have been asking.

The authors of this book wanted to clarify RTI for busy principals and other school leaders in a way that would add value to other available resources. The information in this book conveys the big picture of RTI and points school leaders to other resources useful to filling in the details. It is not meant to be an encyclopedia of RTI. It is not geared to any one school level; elementary, middle, and high school principals will find it helpful. We acknowledge up front that there is no one right way to work within an RTI framework. However, there are some counterproductive ways that we shall point out.

This book was written from a professional development perspective. It is not just a book to read, but also an opportunity to reflect on the subject of RTI and develop action plans suitable to your setting. As we would invite you to do in a workshop format, we encourage you to interact with the text and take the opportunity to respond when prompted to do so. By engaging with the text and using it to engage others in conversations around RTI, you will learn a great deal more and have a basis for making informed decisions about your work with RTI.

The content is geared to school leaders at different levels of familiarity with RTI and stages of implementation. It is divided into three main parts: Understanding RTI, Launching an RTI Initiative at Your School, and Refining an RTI Initiative at Your School. Each part is organized into chapters revolving around practical questions and contains application scenarios in elementary, middle, and high schools, as well as suggested resources.

A clarification of terms at the outset may be helpful:

1. We use the term "Response to Intervention" because this term seems to be used most frequently. We prefer the term "Responsiveness to Intervention" because it conveys more clearly what is involved in the process. RTI looks at how responsive students are to instruction and intervention, not just whether they respond.

2. We recognize that educators from a variety of disciplines use the terms "instruction" and "intervention" differently. We use "intervention" to mean work that exceeds that which can be done by a general classroom teacher in the routine implementation of curriculum, even with differentiated instruction. Intervention can be carried out by a whole host of people, including the classroom teacher, but it will be in addition to differentiated instruction.

3. When we use "instructional support personnel" we include all educators who are not general classroom teachers; e.g., reading specialists or coaches, special education teachers, speech-language pathologists, school psychologists, and others.

It is our hope that this book will provide the impetus for school leaders to begin or continue an RTI initiative that can provide the framework to operationalize the belief that all children and adolescents can learn. Most essentially we hope that it encourages principals and other school leaders to engage in dialog with stakeholders, including staff and parents, to chart a productive course for RTI in their buildings.

Part 1

Understanding Response
to Intervention (RTI)

Advance Organizer

In this part you will learn information to help you understand what RTI is all about. This part provides answers to the following questions:

- What are various organizations' definitions and descriptions of RTI?
- What are the historical and legal roots of RTI?
- What variations/iterations of RTI have been implemented?

The purpose of this part is to provide you with background knowledge about RTI, to either build or expand your RTI schema. Hopefully, this information will lead you to a better understanding of the process so that you can make an informed decision about launching an RTI initiative or refining one already underway.

Chapter 1:

How Do Key Organizations Define and Describe RTI?

When discussing RTI, it is important to realize that RTI is not a one-size-fits-all model for educational reform. Indeed it is not a model at all. Rather, it is a framework to guide educators' efforts to help all children and adolescents achieve their full potential. Depending on the needs of your school, as well as its size, grade levels, personnel, and resources available, the structures and processes of RTI may vary. However, at the heart of RTI is the common goal of helping all students achieve high standards. Several organizations have either defined or described RTI from their perspective. In this section we will present selected definitions and descriptions to give you an orientation to critical elements of RTI. We will address the organizations in alphabetical order.

RTI Definitions and Descriptions

International Reading Association (IRA)

The International Reading Association (IRA) Web site, in the Focus on Response to Intervention (RTI) section, states that "Response to Intervention aims to prevent unnecessary assignment to special education. With RTI, low-performing children are offered intense, individualized academic intervention. Student progress is monitored to see if response to this intervention yields adequate academic growth" (n.d., p. 1).

In addition, the following IRA perspective is reflected in *New Roles in Response to Intervention: Creating Success for Schools and Children—The Role of Reading Specialists in the RTI Process* (IRA, 2006):

> RTI will allow struggling students to receive effective reading interventions early, rather than the to (sic) "wait-to-fail" model currently in practice. RTI is an effort to address the significant percentage of students—up to 40%, according to the President's Commission on Excellence in Special Education—whose reading problems place them in special education classes. Moreover, early reading failure is often a contributing factor in misbehavior that may lead to further special education referrals. (p. 20)

In the same IRA document, further description of RTI includes:

> RTI is a component of comprehensive assessment. Assessment, observation, and curriculum records generated by this early intervention process can be used in making learning-disabled designation decisions. But the RTI process does not necessarily lead to a learning disability designation. Rather, RTI is an effort to avoid an unnecessary learning disability designation by giving the student precise scientifically based reading help much earlier in the game. The teacher's documentation of intervention and progress monitoring is useful information for moving a child to the next appropriate level of help. (IRA, 2006, p. 20)

The IRA roles paper also highlights that professional development, collaboration, leadership, and ongoing consultation regarding student needs are also necessary within the RTI process. In addition, an important point is made that screening for instructional strategies cannot be used as a referral for special education.

National Association of State Directors of Special Education (NASDSE)

According to the National Association of State Directors of Special Education (NASDSE), in their publication, *Response to Intervention: Blueprints for Implementation: School Building Level* (2008, p. 1):

> Response to Intervention (RtI) is the practice of providing high quality instruction and interventions matched to student need, monitoring progress frequently to make decisions about changes in instruction or goals and applying student response data to important educational decisions. RtI should be applied to decisions in general, remedial and special education, creating a well-integrated system of instruction/intervention guided by student outcome data.
>
> > Student outcome data are crucial to:
> > – make accurate decisions about the effectiveness of general and remedial education instruction/interventions;
> > – undertake early identification/intervention with academic and behavioral problems;
> > – prevent unnecessary and excessive identification of students with disabilities;
> > – make decisions about eligibility for special programs, including special education; and
> > – determine individual education programs and deliver and evaluate special education services.

Additionally, Batsche et al., as cited in the NASDSE publication (2008, p. 3), offers a working definition of RTI:

> ...the practice of (1) providing high quality instruction/intervention matched to student needs and (2) using learning rate over time and level of performance to (3) make important educational decisions. These components of RtI are essential to the development of a successful RtI implementation strategy.

1. HIGH QUALITY INSTRUCTION/ INTERVENTION is defined as instruction or intervention matched to student need that has been demonstrated through scientific research and practice to produce high learning rates for *most* students. Individual responses to even the best instruction/intervention are variable. Selection and implementation of scientifically based instruction/intervention markedly increases the probability of, but does not guarantee positive individual response. Therefore, *individual* response is assessed in RtI and modifications to instruction/intervention and goals are made depending on results with *individual* students.

2. LEARNING RATE AND LEVEL OF PERFORMANCE are the primary sources of information used in ongoing decision making. Learning rate refers to a student's individual growth in achievement or behavior competencies over time. Level of performance refers to a student's relative standing on some dimension of achievement/ performance compared to expected performance (either criterion- or norm-referenced). Learning rates and levels of performance vary significantly across students. Most students with achievement or behavioral challenges respond positively to explicit and intense instruction/interventions. Decisions about the use of more or less intense interventions are made using information on learning rate and level. More intense interventions may occur in general education classrooms or pull-out programs supported by general, compensatory, or special education funding.

3. IMPORTANT EDUCATIONAL DECISIONS about intensity and the likely duration of interventions are based on individual student response to instruction across multiple tiers of intervention. Decisions about the necessity of more intense interventions, including eligibility for special education and/or exit from special education or other services, are informed by data on learning rate and level.

NASDE also highlights additional RTI elements in their *Response to Intervention: NASDSE and CASE White Paper on RTI* (NASDE, 2006). The additional RTI elements found in this document are: universal screening, early identification, professional development, and progress monitoring.

National Center for Learning Disabilities (NCLD)

According to NCLD's Parent Advocacy Brief, *A Parent's Guide to Response-to-Intervention* (Cortiella, 2006, p.1):

> The RTI process is a multi-step approach to providing services and interventions to students who struggle with learning at increasing levels of intensity. The progress students make at each stage of intervention is closely monitored. Results of this monitoring are used to make decisions about the need for further research-based instruction and/or intervention in general education, in special education or both. The RTI process has the potential to limit the amount of academic failure that any student experiences and to increase the accuracy of special education evaluations. Its use could also reduce the number of children who are mistakenly identified as having learning disabilities when their learning problems are actually

due to cultural differences or lack of adequate instruction. Information and data gathered by an RTI process can lead to earlier identification of children who have true disabilities and are in need of special education services.

Additionally, in the July 2005 edition of *LD News*, within the Research Roundup section, NCLD's Horowitz (2005, p.1) reports that:

> While there is no single recommended approach to implementing an RTI model, there are a number of basic features that approaches have in common:
>
> - students first receive high-quality instruction in general education settings
> - to the greatest extent possible, all instruction is research-based
> - general education professionals and other teaching staff share active roles in student instruction and in collecting data on student performance
> - student progress is monitored across the curriculum not just on specific isolated skills
> - student progress monitoring is ongoing (not just a snapshot of scores at a particular point in time)
> - the RTI approach is well documented and is seamlessly integrated into schoolwide practice

National Research Center on Learning Disabilities (NRCLD)

The National Research Center on Learning Disabilities (NRCLD), states in *What is RTI?* (n.d., p. 1) that:

> Responsiveness to intervention is an education model that promotes early identification of students who may be at risk for learning difficulties. RTI, which may be *one component* in the process a school uses to determine whether a student has a specific learning disability, often involves tiers of increasingly intense levels of service for students. Most students will thrive in general education classrooms. For those who don't, a second tier will focus additional attention on the academic area in which the child struggles. More tiers may be available for students with greater needs.
>
> RTI is a valuable construct because of its potential utility in providing appropriate learning experiences for *all* students and for its use in the early identification of students at risk for academic failure. Students benefit when their current levels of skill and ability are aligned with the instructional and curricular choices provided within their classroom. When a mismatch occurs, student learning and outcomes are lowered. For some students, typical classroom instruction is appropriate and meets their needs, but for others, success is not easy. The RTI hypothesis is that the earlier these floundering students are identified and provided appropriate instruction, the higher the likelihood they can be successful and maintain their class placement.

Additionally, NRCLD in their RTI manual highlights six elements of RTI service delivery models: schoolwide screening, progress monitoring, tiered service delivery, data-based decision making, parent involvement, and fidelity of implementation (Johnson, Mellard, Fuchs, & McKnight, 2006).

An NRCLD paper, *Understanding Responsiveness to Intervention in Disabilities Determination*, written by Mellard (2004) lists the following core features and attributes of RTI:

Core Features:

- High-quality research-based classroom instruction
- Student assessment with classroom focus
- Universal screening of academics and behavior
- Continuous progress monitoring of students
- Implementation of appropriate research-based interventions
- Progress monitoring during interventions (effectiveness)
- Teaching behavior fidelity measures

Attributes:

- Multiple tiers
- Differentiated curriculum
- Instruction from other resource professionals at higher tiers
- Interventions with varied, frequency, duration, and time
- Placement decisions either categorical or noncategorical

Common Elements in Definitions and Descriptions

From the various definitions and descriptions of RTI, common elements emerge:

RTI COMMON ELEMENTS AT A GLANCE
Student Outcome Measures
High-Quality (Scientifically Based) Instruction/Intervention
Progress Monitoring/Formative Assessment
Data-Based Decision Making
Educational Decision Making Based on Responsiveness to Instruction/Intervention
Instruction/Intervention Intensity Changes Based on Performance

Other common elements not captured in all the examples cited above include universal screening to identify struggling learners and the use of tiers as an infrastructure to organize levels of intensity.

What RTI Is and What it Is Not

There is no one framework for RTI. It changes based on the school environment, culture, and student learning needs. This lack of uniform structure likely contributes to misunderstanding about the RTI construct. Table 1.1 clarifies boundaries of the RTI framework.

Purposes of RTI

The purposes of RTI may vary with the implementing agency. Broadly, RTI has three purposes: prevention of learning failure, intervention to ameliorate learning difficulties, and determination of learning disabilities. It should be noted that, in many school districts, RTI is not yet being used for determination of learning disabilities.

Prevention

The prevention aspect of the RTI framework begins with high-quality core instruction to ensure that any problems students may be experiencing are not related to ineffective teaching practices. For students having academic or behavioral problems, the idea is to promote success before a cycle of failure begins. RTI seeks to intervene before student gaps in learning become so large that they are labeled with a learning disability, often times needlessly. Prevention is addressed within an RTI framework by employing screening of all students. Student progress is then continuously monitored throughout the school year.

Intervention

Once a student is identified as not meeting predetermined benchmarks after receiving high-quality core instruction, additional supports are provided to the student. Academic issues, such as literacy and math, and behavioral issues may be addressed. This instruction is designed to meet the needs of the student. Initial intervention often occurs in small groups and may take place in the regular education classroom or elsewhere. The person who leads small group instruction may be the teacher, speech-language pathologist, resource specialist, reading specialist, or other qualified professional unique to each school's environment. The student's responsiveness to this intervention is closely monitored through data collection and analysis. The frequency and duration of interventions can be altered depending on student progress. Then, if the student is showing little progress, the intervention program may increase in intensity to focus on individual needs. If insufficient progress is seen after a predetermined period of time, the student may be referred for further evaluation and possible special education placement.

Table 1.1. What RTI Is and What it Is Not	
RTI IS an approach:	**RTI IS NOT** an approach:
That allows students to move freely among tiers of instruction/intervention.	That is lock-step, where students must go through successive steps to get to the next.
That involves a multistep and multifaceted process to improve student learning.	That is "one-size-fits-all."
Providing prevention of failure and intervention, when they need it, for all students who struggle with learning.	Providing help for the student only once they are identified as having a learning disability.
Providing interventions in general education, compensatory education, special education, or all of the above.	Providing services only in one setting.
For students who struggle with learning in all educational settings.	Only for students with learning disabilities.
Providing increasing levels of intensity depending on student response.	Providing a fixed level of intensity for all students.
Providing different stages (tiers) of instruction depending on student need.	Providing only whole-group learning opportunities that are not individualized or based on student need.
Involving continuous progress monitoring.	Involving end-of-year assessment alone to gauge student progress.
Utilizing progress monitoring data to shape future instruction.	Utilizing curricula scope and sequence in isolation to guide instructional approaches.
Providing research-based instruction.	Providing teaching approaches based on teacher preference.
Providing differentiated instruction.	Providing only whole-group classroom teaching.
Used to improve student learning.	Used only for special education identification and placement.
Implemented in many iterations depending on school, resources, and goals.	Implemented with the same methods, schedule, service providers, and framework in each school.
Incorporating fidelity measures into teaching, assessment, and intervention.	Disregarding consistency in teaching practices, assessment, or intervention.
Dependent upon collaboration among professionals (both inside and outside the building) as well as parents regarding student needs.	Dependent upon one person to make decisions about students.
Encouraging high-quality professional development to learn research-based approaches.	Relying on "one-shot" workshops.

Determination of Learning Disabilities

Within an RTI framework, when a student is not sufficiently responsive to high-quality core instruction and interventions in subsequent tiers within general or compensatory education, it may indicate the need for special education services. In such a case, the data gathered during progress monitoring throughout preliminary tiers may be used as part of the process for determination of a learning disability. Hence, lack of responsiveness to intervention can be used as part of a comprehensive evaluation process. Federal law no longer requires the application of a formula indicating a discrepancy between intelligence (IQ) and achievement as a component for determination of learning disabilities.

Although different districts may place greater emphasis on one or more purposes, in actuality the purposes should be integrated in a systematic approach to meeting all students needs, as depicted in Figure 1.1.

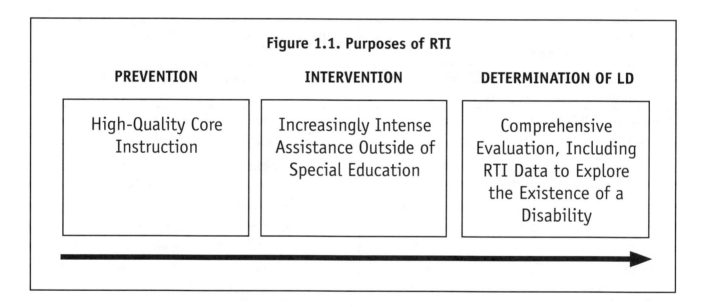

Figure 1.1. Purposes of RTI

PREVENTION	INTERVENTION	DETERMINATION OF LD
High-Quality Core Instruction	Increasingly Intense Assistance Outside of Special Education	Comprehensive Evaluation, Including RTI Data to Explore the Existence of a Disability

The Process of RTI

As mentioned earlier, RTI is not a model. It is a multifaceted process that is designed to improve the learning outcomes for all students. As such, there are many facets which have to be considered. In the process of implementing RTI, you may encounter stumbling blocks; this may be a new path you are embarking on and each building will have its unique characteristics. If you think of RTI as a process, you will learn to approach the concept with an open mind. You will realize that it is not going to be implemented quickly, run smoothly, and change student outcomes immediately. You will realize that you will learn more about yourself, your school, your teachers, and your students as you seize your school's unique opportunities. Keep in mind that RTI involves:

- **A schoolwide improvement process that addresses student needs and Adequate Yearly Progress (AYP)**

  RTI is a conceptual framework that can address student learning needs targeted by your school improvement plan. It can be the structure that helps you to meet AYP goals set forth by the No Child Left Behind (NCLB) legislation. RTI adoption goals should not be separate from school improvement plan goals.

- **A process that includes general education, compensatory education, and special education**

  The beauty of the RTI construct is that all programs and services can be integrated into it. Therefore, general education, compensatory education, and special education programs and services, too frequently implemented in silos at the school level, can form a unitary system for meeting students' needs.

- **A process for elementary, middle, and high schools**

  Although many current RTI initiatives focus on elementary schools, RTI can be implemented at all grade levels. Because middle and high schools are not just larger versions of elementary schools, RTI initiatives may take different forms at secondary levels. However, core elements of RTI can and should be retained.

- **A process that should align with current district and state priorities**

  Implementation of RTI should be congruent with the current priorities of the district and state. Some schools will be free to design their own iterations of RTI, while others will be asked to follow district or state designs.

- **A process that incorporates differentiated instruction**

  RTI begins with differentiated instruction to improve student learning, no matter what level of success a student is achieving. Differentiated instruction includes the ability to adjust the content of what is taught, the process by which it is taught, and the means by which it is assessed. The focus on differentiated instruction exemplifies the student-centered approach of the RTI process and the belief that all children and adolescents can learn. RTI focuses on the ability to adjust the instruction to the individual student rather that requiring the student to adjust to the instruction.

- **A process that incorporates research-based instruction/intervention**

  High-quality, research-based instructional methods are used within all components of RTI. This evidence-based practice approach ensures the best education for children and adolescents.

- **A process that often includes a multitiered approach**

  RTI approaches employ levels or tiers of instruction/intervention along a continuum of intensity. Tiered systems provide guidelines regarding changes in instruction/intervention across the tiers to achieve student success. A good tiered system permits flexible movement across tiers, depending on the supports students need at a particular time.

- **A process that uses data to make instructional decisions**

  Ongoing progress monitoring is used to evaluate students' responsiveness to the instruction or intervention they are receiving in the tiers. These data are used to make adjustments in the frequency, duration, or methods of teaching to facilitate student learning.

- **A process that requires leadership, collaboration, and buy-in from all levels**

  RTI is not a single package that can be purchased and implemented all at once. It is a process that will take time, requiring leadership from administrators and buy-in from all stakeholders. General and special education teachers, paraprofessionals, instructional support staff (e.g., reading specialists, speech-language pathologists, school psychologists, guidance counselors, occupational therapists, physical therapists, educational audiologists, social workers, and others), and parents must understand RTI and support its adoption.

- **A process that requires a commitment to ongoing professional development**

  It is likely for new roles to be undertaken in the RTI process among professionals at the school; for example, data collection and analysis. Teachers and other staff members must be prepared for these new roles and for working together to implement them. More than one or two workshops will be necessary to set up professionals for success. Ongoing, job-embedded professional development is an essential part of the process.

Scenarios

Elementary School

A K-5 school has implemented universal screening in reading for all students at each grade level three times per year. The students who do not meet benchmarks are given small-group interventions that are designed to meet their needs. Each student's progress is monitored regularly and the interventions are modified as necessary. Teachers are implementing instruction and interventions with fidelity, as determined by the principal. This school has begun to implement the RTI process.

Middle School

A middle school with grades 6-8 has earned poor state achievement scores in literacy areas over the last 2 years. Teachers think their students are lazy and unmotivated. Students are assessed only during state achievement tests. The students who struggle in many classes throughout the year are referred for special education testing, because the teachers think there must be something wrong with these students. For the most part, teachers are using a whole-group instructional model where lecture is the primary teaching mode. Very few small-group, individualized activities are used in the classroom. Students are expected to learn what's being taught to the class regardless of their level of current knowledge. This example illustrates a school that has not yet begun to implement the RTI process to improve student learning.

High School

A high school with grades 9-12 has just implemented a universal screening system to assess students in literacy, math, and behavioral components. A student's grades had recently fallen, but his literacy and math screening measures reflected adequate progress. A checklist was used to rate behaviors of the student. The student had not received any behavior referrals. Teachers reported he was not disruptive in class and paid attention. The aspect that caused concern in the behavioral screening was the number of absences reported. The student had 10 absences each semester, in his first- through third-period classes, for two consecutive semesters. A meeting among the guidance counselor, content-area teachers, student, and parent revealed that this student had started a job at the beginning of the school year. The student worked from 7 pm to 11 pm three nights per week (weekdays) at a local grocery store. The student reported that he was missing class because he was tired in the morning and "just wanted to sleep in." The mother reported that she and her husband left for work prior to the time the student left for school and didn't know their son was missing so much school. During the meeting the student acknowledged that his work was interfering with his studies and that he should talk to his employer about working two weekend evenings and only one weekday evening so that he could concentrate on schoolwork and be rested in the mornings. The behavioral screening keyed in on an issue that might have otherwise gone unnoticed.

Resources

RTI WEB VIDEOS Five 90 minute free web casts: • *Why Implement RtI?* • *What Is RtI?* • *Administrative Issues in RtI* • *Instruction in RtI Systems* • *Getting Started With RtI*	Council of Administrators of Special Education: http://www.casecec.org/rti.htm or Response to Intervention: Training for California Educators http://www4.scoe.net/rti/programs.cfm?menuChoice=3
RTI VIDEOS **Behavioral Models:** • *The Implementation of Behavior Instruction in the Total School* • *Positive Unified Behavior Support: A Model of School-Wide Positive Behavior Support* **Reading Models:** • *School-Wide Reading Model*	Office of Special Education Programs (OSEP) Technical Center on Positive Behavioral Interventions and Supports http://www.pbis.org/PBIS_videos.htm

References

Cortiella, C. (2006). *Parent advocacy brief: A parent's guide to Response-to-Intervention.* National Center for Learning Disabilities. Retrieved May 15, 2008, from http://www.ncld.org/images/stories/downloads/parent_center/rti_final.pdf

Horowitz, S. H. (2005, July). Response to Intervention: A primer. *LD News.* Research Roundup Section. Retrieved March 23, 2008, from http://www.ncld.org/content/view/598/

International Reading Association. (n.d.). *Focus on Response to Intervention.* Retrieved June 15, 2008, from http://www.reading.org/resources/issues/focus_rti.html

International Reading Association. (2006). *New roles in Response to Intervention: Creating success for schools and children – The role of reading specialists in the RTI process.* Retrieved March 1, 2008, from http://www.ira.org/downloads/resources/rti_role_definitions.pdf

Johnson, E., Mellard, D. F., Fuchs, D., & McKnight, M. A. (2006). *Responsiveness to Intervention (RTI): How to do it.* Lawrence, KS: National Research Center on Learning Disabilities. Retrieved March 1, 2008, from http://www.nrcld.org/rti_manual/index.html

Mellard, D. (2004). *Understanding Responsiveness to Intervention in learning disabilities determination.* Retrieved June 16, 2008, from www.nrcld.org/about/publications/papers/mellard.html

National Association of State Directors of Special Education. (2008). *Response to Intervention: Blueprints for implementation – School building level.* Retrieved May 15, 2008, from http://www.nasdse.org/Portals/0/SCHOOL.pdf

National Association of State Directors of Special Education, & Council of Administrators of Special Education. (2006). *Response to Intervention.* Arlington, VA: Council for Exceptional Children. Retrieved March 1, 2008, from http://www.nasdse.org/Portals/0/Documents/Download%20Publications/RtIAnAdministratorsPerspective1-06.pdf

National Research Center on Learning Disabilities (NRCLD). (n.d.) *What is RTI?* Retrieved June 16, 2008, from http://www.nrcld.org/topics/rti.html

Reflection

Answer these questions to gauge your awareness of RTI.

1. Are you hearing more and more about RTI at your state-, district-, or local-level meetings?

    ❏ Yes   ❏ No

2. Are you discussing individualized, research-based, data-driven decision making with progress monitoring (key elements of RTI) to improve student learning at your district, or building level?

    ❏ Yes   ❏ No

3. Are you noticing an increasing number of RTI articles in national organization publications or on national association Web sites?

    ❏ Yes   ❏ No

4. What elements from the RTI definitions and descriptions noted in this section are used in your district or at your school?

    _____

    _____

    _____

    _____

    _____

    _____

    _____

    _____

    _____

    _____

    _____

    _____

    _____

    _____

    _____

Chapter 2:

What Are the Historical and Legal Roots of RTI?

∇ **The Seeds of RTI**
∇ **Significance of NCLB**
∇ **Significance of IDEA**
∇ **Scenarios**
∇ **Resources**
∇ **References**
∇ **Reflection**

RTI is not a new concept. Some schools and districts have been using components of this approach for years. Recent focus on RTI may in part be due to the increasing accountability for student learning placed on schools by federal legislation, including No Child Left Behind (NCLB) and the Individuals with Disabilities Education Act (IDEA). We note up front that the term "Response to Intervention" does not appear in law, although IDEA alludes to responding to intervention in determination of learning disabilities. There are components of RTI, however, that are rooted in federal legislation. Below, we'll examine the historical and legal roots of RTI.

The Seeds of RTI

Over a decade ago, IRA (International Reading Association) became concerned about the increasing numbers of students that were being identified as having learning disabilities because they were having difficulty learning to read. IRA was concerned because many of these students who were being identified as poor readers had not received more intensive or expert instruction in how to become better readers (Allington & Walmsley, 1995).

In 1998, IRA lobbied to have IDEA amended to include at least 1 year of expert, intensive reading intervention before a student could be referred for special education evaluation. Although this provision was not implemented, it did plant the seeds for future legislation.

In 2004, the organization again addressed the idea of overidentification of students with learning disabilities during the IDEA reauthorization. There was widespread concern about the methods used to determine eligibility because a wide gap was needed before a student could be categorized as having a disability. This meant a significant delay in the ability to access services to help students succeed.

Along other lines, for many years researchers and practitioners in the field of learning disabilities have been discussing the determination of learning disabilities. Central to the controversy has been the use of a discrepancy model requiring a gap between intellectual functioning and academic achievement. Traditionally the IQ-achievement discrepancy model has been used to qualify a student as having a learning disability. In this approach, a measure of intellectual ability is compared with a measure of academic performance. Discrepancy between these two areas is often the key qualifying factor for receiving services within the learning disabilities category. However, specific criteria often differed from state to state or district to district; for example, differing assessment measures and differing gaps between intellectual ability and achievement. These differences led to inequities in provision of services to struggling students.

In 2001, the Office of Special Education Programs funded the National Research Center for Learning Disabilities (NRCLD) to conduct research on the identification of learning disabilities, formulate implementation recommendations, disseminate findings, and provide technical assistance to national, state, and local constituencies. This center has engaged professionals in ongoing dialogue about alternative means for identifying students with learning disabilities, including the use of a Responsiveness to Intervention approach.

Significance of NCLB

NCLB (2001) [PL 107-15] was developed from Title 1 of the Elementary and Secondary Education Act (ESEA) of 1965. Title 1 of ESEA was designed to improve the academic achievement of students from disadvantaged backgrounds. The main focus of this legislation is to ensure that all children and adolescents receive access to a high-quality education and to narrow the achievement gap between students from disadvantaged backgrounds and their peers. Contained within the legislation are various components of the RTI framework, although reference to RTI *per se* does not appear in the law. Let's look at some of the specific NCLB aims that relate to RTI:

Improving Academic Achievement of All Students

> ...Holding schools, local educational agencies, and States accountable for **improving the academic achievement of all students**, and identifying and turning around low-performing schools that have failed to provide a high-quality education to their students, while providing alternatives to students in such schools to enable the students to receive a high-quality education. (NCLB, 2001, Sec 1001[4], p.16) (Emphasis added.)

Accountability for Meeting Standards

> ...Improving and strengthening **accountability**, teaching, and learning by **using State assessment systems** designed to ensure that students are meeting challenging State academic achievement and content standards and increasing achievement overall, but especially for the disadvantaged. (NCLB, 2001, Sec 1001[6], p. 16) (Emphasis added.)

Included in accountability requirements is the requirement that schools must meet **Adequate Yearly Progress**.

> Each State plan shall demonstrate...what constitutes adequate yearly progress of the State, and of all public elementary schools, secondary schools, and local educational agencies in the State, toward enabling all public elementary school and secondary school students to meet the State's student academic achievement standards, while working toward the goal of narrowing the achievement gaps in the State, local educational agencies, and schools. (NCLB, 2001, Sec 1111[b] [2] [B], p. 22)

Scientifically Based Instructional Strategies

...Providing children an enriched and accelerated educational program, including the use of school wide programs or additional services that increase the amount and quality of instructional time; promoting school wide reform and ensuring the access of children to effective, **scientifically based instructional strategies** and challenging academic content. (NCLB, 2001, Sec 1001[8] [9], p. 16) (Emphasis added.)

Professional Development

...Significantly elevating the quality of instruction by providing staff in participating schools with substantial opportunities for **professional development**. (NCLB, 2001, Sec 1001[10], p.16) (Emphasis added.)

Parental Opportunities

...Affording **parents substantial and meaningful opportunities** to participate in the education of their children. (NCLB, 2001, Sec 1001[12], p.16) (Emphasis added.)

Flexibility to Schools and Teachers

...Providing greater decision making authority and **flexibility to schools and teachers** in exchange for greater responsibility for student performance. (NCLB, 2001, Sec 1001[7], p. 16) (Emphasis added.)

These NCLB elements supply the roots of RTI. Through an RTI framework, schools can facilitate access for all students to the kind high-quality education NCLB intended.

Significance of IDEA

The Individuals with Disabilities Education Act of 2004 (IDEA, 2004, PL 108-446) developed from the Education of All Handicapped Children Act of 1975. This law is designed to address the educational needs of students with disabilities and ensure that they receive a free appropriate public education. IDEA 2004 focuses on many elements that are congruent with RTI, including alternatives for determination of learning disabled. Let's examine these RTI roots.

Early Intervening Services—Intervention Before Failing

A portion of IDEA funding may be available to address individual student learning needs through Early Intervening Services. Fifteen percent of funds targeted for students with disabilities may be used in general education interventions for at-risk students who need additional support to succeed in the general education setting. However there are some special considerations on the use of these funds (IDEA 2004, Sec. 613, f). Early Intervening Services funds can also be used for teacher professional development in the area of scientifically based instruction (IDEA 2004, Sec. 613, f, 2, A).

Effective Instruction

IDEA 2004 is clear in its statement that lack of effective instruction is not a reason to be labeled as a student with a disability. Section 614, b, 5, A, states, "…a child shall not be determined to be a child with a disability if the determinant factor for such determination is—(A) lack of appropriate instruction in reading, including in the essential components of reading instruction…" (IDEA, 2004).

IQ-Achievement Discrepancy No Longer Required for Determination of Learning Disabled

An important element of IDEA 2004 is that school districts are no longer required to use a discrepancy formula to determine the existence of learning disabilities. "…A local educational agency shall not be required to take into consideration whether a child has a severe discrepancy between achievement and intellectual ability in oral expression, listening comprehension, written expression, basic reading skill, reading comprehension, mathematical calculation, or mathematical reasoning" (IDEA 2004, Section 614, b, 6, A).

Response to Scientific, Research-Based Intervention

In IDEA 2004, response to scientifically based interventions may be used in determination of learning disabilities. As noted in the following statement, "…In determining whether a child has a specific learning disability, a local educational agency may use a process that determines if the child responds to scientific, research-based intervention as a part of the evaluation procedures…" (Sec. 614, b, 6, B).

Educational Outcomes/Specially Designed Instruction

> The importance of educational outcomes are illustrated in IDEA 2004 in the following provision, The term 'individualized education program' or 'IEP' means a written statement for each child with a disability that is developed, reviewed, and revised in accordance with this section and that includes—(I) a statement of the child's present levels of academic achievement and functional performance, including—(aa) how the child's disability affects the child's involvement and progress in the general education curriculum (Sec. 614, d, 1, A, i).

IDEA 2004 is explicit in the purpose of specially designed instruction. "Specially designed instruction…[is used] (i) To address the unique needs of the child that result from the child's disability, and (ii) To ensure access of the child to the general curriculum, so that he or she can meet the educational standards within the jurisdiction of the public agency that apply to all children" (Sec. 300.39, b, 3, i & ii).

Professional Development

IDEA 2004 emphasizes professional development in its provision that states, "—The local educational agency shall ensure that all personnel necessary to carry out this part are appropriately and adequately prepared…" (Sec. 613, a, 3).

Collaboration and Parental Involvement

IDEA 2004 promotes the ideas of collaboration and parental involvement in the following statement:

…Upon completion of the administration of assessments and other evaluation measures—(A) the determination of whether the child is a child with a disability as defined in section 602(3) and the educational needs of the child shall be made by a team of qualified professionals and the parent of the child…. (IDEA 2004, Sec. 614, b, 4, A)

Another example of the collaborative nature of IDEA 2004 is illustrated in this provision:

…The IEP Team and other qualified professionals, as appropriate, shall—(A) review existing evaluation data on the child, including—(i) evaluations and information provided by the parents of the child; (ii) current classroom-based, local, or State assessments, and classroom-based observations; and (iii) observations by teachers and related services providers…. (IDEA 2004, Sec. 614, c, 1, A, i-iii)

IDEA 2004 has had significant effects on RTI. Schools and school districts may have been using some elements of RTI in the past, but with the legal references that include so many specific RTI components, RTI initiatives are receiving considerable attention.

LEGAL ROOTS AT-A-GLANCE

NCLB
- Improving academic achievement of all students
- Accountability for meeting standards, including the requirement to meet Adequate Yearly Progress (AYP)
- Scientifically based instructional strategies
- Professional development
- Parental opportunities
- Flexibility to schools and teachers

IDEA
- Early intervening services—intervention before failing including professional development for teachers
- Effective instruction
- IQ-Achievement discrepancy no longer required for determination of learning disabilities
- Response to scientific, research-based intervention for determination of learning disabilities
- Educational outcomes/specially designed instruction
- Professional development
- Collaboration and parental involvement

Scenarios

Elementary School

A K-5 school decided they needed professional development on the relationship between classroom design and student learning. This approach was to be taught by a teacher at another school who had success in leading small-group activities that fostered more student interaction. Before moving forward with this professional development, the principal checked on the research base for this approach. He knew that for professional development to be worth the teachers' time and effort and to meet legal requirements it needed to revolve around scientifically based practices.

Middle School

A grade 6-8 school has failed to meet AYP. Desegregation of achievement data reveals that students who are English Language Learners and students of poverty were subgroups that did not meet standards on the state assessment test in reading. The principal has asked the language arts teachers, reading specialist, and speech-language pathologist to work together to identify scientifically based interventions that might be used to help these students in reading.

High School

A 10th-grade student began to do poorly in her classes. She previously had been an average student. In a formative reading assessment given to her entire grade, she performed below expectation. Her low score baffled her English teacher. The teacher wondered whether the student should have small-group intervention, but had reservations because the student had not evidenced problems previously. Due to the teacher's suspicion that there might be more going on with this student than literacy issues, she called the student's mother. Collaboration with the mother in this case revealed that there were family issues at home that were probably interfering with schoolwork. The decision was to watch her grades and re-administer a reading assessment during the next marking period.

Resources

Printables: NCLB Fact Sheets	U.S. Department of Education Web site http://www.ed.gov/news/opeds/factsheets/index.html?src=az
Video Clip: Early Intervening Services/ Response To Intervention (RTI) Video Clip *Lecture style video	U.S. Department of Education Web site: IDEA 2004 Information link http://idea.ed.gov/explore/view/p/%2Croot%2Cdynamic%2CVideoClips%2C16%2C
Printables: Dialogue Guides for IDEA. IDEA regulations by topic in handout form.	IDEA Partnership http://www.ideapartnership.org/oseppage.cfm?pageid=36
Video Series: *Building the Legacy: Individuals with Disabilities Education Act Amendments of 2004*. NICHCY's Building the Legacy: A Training Curriculum on IDEA 2004.	National Dissemination Center for Children with Disabilities (NICHCY) http://www.nichcy.org/training/contents.asp#description

References

Allington, F. L., & Walmsley, S. A. (Eds). (1995). *No quick fix.* New York: Teachers College Press.

Individuals With Disabilities Education Improvement Act. (2004). Public Law 108-446. Retrieved March 1, 2008, from http://idea.ed.gov/explore/view/p/%2Croot%2Cstatute%2C

No Child Left Behind Act. (2001). Public Law 107-15. Retrieved March 1, 2008, from http://www.ed.gov/policy/elsec/leg/esea02/index.html

Reflection

Answer these questions to gauge your exposure to the links between RTI and federal law.

1. Are you hearing about the relationship between RTI and NCLB, RTI and IDEA through national, state, or district meetings?

   ❏ Yes   ❏ No

2. Are you discussing the legal roots of RTI in NCLB and IDEA with central office staff, other building-level administrators, or teachers?

   ❏ Yes   ❏ No

3. Are you noticing an increasing number of articles in your professional publications or on your professional association Web sites about the relationship between RTI and NCLB, RTI and IDEA?

   ❏ Yes   ❏ No

4. With which legal roots of NCLB and IDEA are you most familiar?

   _____

   _____

   _____

   _____

   _____

   _____

   _____

   _____

   _____

   _____

   _____

   _____

   _____

   _____

   _____

   _____

Chapter 3:

What Iterations of RTI Have Been Implemented?

As we have discussed, the RTI process may look different from school to school. The framework can differ, depending on school grade levels and the differing needs of the students. Cultural and socioeconomic factors can also affect design, as can availability of personnel and resources. Although iterations differ, most RTI approaches employ a tiered approach. Below, we'll briefly highlight some of the tiered approaches that have been studied. More in-depth explanation of the tiered approach will be provided in Part 2.

Tiered Approaches

The term "tiers" refers to levels along a continuum of intensity for instruction and intervention. Most RTI initiatives employ tiers, although they may not use that term. Several different structures have been studied.

Two-Tiered Structure

Two-tiered models operate under the assumption that the general education curriculum (Tier 1) provides high-quality instruction at the appropriate levels for most students. In this structure it is believed that most students can succeed in the general education environment. Tier 2 becomes the level where a student receives extra, individualized, research-based, and intensive help, as a student with a disability, if he or she is not progressing well in the general academic environment. According to Fuchs, Fuchs, & Compton (2004), "students are identified as LD when their response to generally effective instruction (i.e., instruction to which most children respond) is dramatically inferior to that of their peers" (p. 216). Fuchs et al., go on to state, "the basic assumption is that RTI can differentiate between two explanations of low achievement: poor instruction versus disability" (p. 216).

Three-Tiered Structure

This is the most widespread framework for RTI. This model assumes that most students can be successful in the general education curriculum. When a student is not making adequate progress in the general education environment, as judged by academic performance and other screening measures, the student is given more assistance in the hope that he or she will reach the predetermined school benchmarks. This assistance is provided in Tier 2. At this level, the intervention may be carried out in small groups for a specific amount of time. Progress is monitored routinely. If the intervention is working, and the student achieves targeted benchmarks, he or she may stop receiving the small group help. If on the other hand the student is not making progress, he or she may receive more frequent intervention or intervention of longer duration. The student may be referred for Tier 3 services—more intensive sessions that may or may not occur within the classroom. Often, specially trained personnel work with the student at this level to help him or her succeed. Within this level is the option for referral for special education evaluation, if the student has not responded to the various interventions over a predetermined period of time. At any time within the intervention process, the student may move back and forth between tiers, depending on level of performance and mastery of skills.

Four-Tiered Structure

Ikeda and Gustafson (as cited in Fuchs & Fuchs, 2006) discussed a four-tiered structure that has been used in an Iowa school district. This school district called the variations in treatment "levels" instead of tiers. This is a problem-solving model in which Level 1 involves a teacher/parent conference to address an issue. Level 2 involves a team of professionals within the school collaborating to discuss the individual student issue. The team helps the teacher select and monitor the intervention. Level 3 is where the students who were unsuccessful in Level 2 progress to special assistance from special educators to adjust, refine, and coordinate the intervention's implementation. Ikeda, Tilly, Stumme, Volmer, and Allison (1996) stated these special educators included "School Psychologists, Instructional Consultants, School Social Workers, Speech and Language Pathologists, Early Childhood Consultants, Itinerant Hearing and Vision Teachers, Occupational Therapists, Physical Therapists, Nurses, Work Experience Coordinators, Adaptive Physical Education Teachers, an Assistive Technology Team, Educational Trainers, and Parent Liaisons" (p. 231). If the various problem-solving intervention approaches are not successful at Level 3, special education assistance and due process protections are considered at Level 4 (Fuchs & Fuchs, 2006).

Five-Tiered Structure

Multitiered structures with more than four levels are generally variations in a three- or four-tiered approach with tiers broken into smaller parts. The consistent component among the tiered structures is that Level 1 is the general education level and the level where most students' needs are met. As the levels increase in number, the interventions become more individualized and intensive. In addition, lower student-teacher ratios often result, more specialized personnel become involved, and more frequent and extensive progress monitoring and data collection are employed. As with the other tiered structures, student movement across levels is flexible, based on progress.

Intervention Approaches

There are two basic types of intervention approaches: the problem-solving approach and the standard treatment protocol (Fuchs & Fuchs, 2006). There may be combinations of these two approaches, as well.

Problem-Solving Approach

The problem-solving approach is essentially a collaborative effort to "…identify and analyze problems and to help the teacher select, implement, and monitor the effectiveness of an intervention" (Fuchs & Fuchs, 2006, p. 94). This approach initially focuses on providing help within the classroom setting. It relies heavily on student progress data to assess the effectiveness of the intervention. The treatment approach varies from student to student.

Standard Treatment Protocol

The standard treatment protocol is often used because of its more specific design. In this approach, there are more specific and prescriptive interventions within a treatment category. Often the treatment is set in content, duration, and frequency. Students who are unresponsive to the treatment are immediately moved to the next level or tier of intervention or to a different treatment. "But if they show insufficient progress at Tier 2, a disability is suspected and further evaluation is warranted" (Fuchs & Fuchs, 2006, p. 95). In this design, the treatment approach shows far less variability among students than is seen in problem-solving models.

Personnel Involved

Essentially everyone at the building level is involved in the various approaches to RTI. Classroom teachers, special education teachers, speech-language pathologists, reading specialists, reading coaches, school psychologists, administrators, occupational therapists, physical therapists, educational audiologists, librarians, parents, office personnel, and even outside professionals may play a role in RTI. RTI is a collaborative process that invites input from everyone to formulate the best plan to address the learning needs of all students. With RTI, personnel within a school may find themselves expanding their roles and responsibilities as well as their ways of thinking about education. Schools may have to consider realignment of personnel to accomplish associated tasks; for example, the data-driven nature of RTI will require personnel to manage data.

The Role of Special Education

Referral for special education services remains an option within all RTI iterations. However, special education referral is made only after interventions have not resulted in student learning success. Student success in these cases is judged by ongoing data collection during the frequently monitored and modified intervention process. Students who do not respond to increasingly intensive interventions may proceed to a comprehensive evaluation. If the student is identified as having a disability at this point, an Individualized Education Plan (IEP) will be developed. After the IEP has been generated, the student will be provided with even more intensive intervention called "specially designed instruction." Progress continues to be monitored regularly, and often more frequently.

Scenarios

Elementary School

A reading specialist in an elementary school used to pull children out of their classes for reading assistance. The teacher never had the opportunity to observe the interaction of the reading specialist and students. As the elementary school began to implement the RTI process, the reading specialist began providing instruction in the classroom to small groups of students. The teacher learned new ways to adjust her teaching style to help each of these students. The collaboration between the teacher and the reading specialist fostered open dialogue about other students and intervention strategies.

Middle School

A grade 6-8 school began to implement the RTI process. Many students fell below grade-level benchmarks on the initial schoolwide screening for literacy and behavior. Additionally, it was noted that several of these students were also receiving speech-language services from the speech-language pathologist (SLP) and were on behavioral support plans from the school psychologist. The SLP had been using a pull-out service delivery model. The psychologist had been meeting with the students once every 2 weeks, also pulling them out. As a result of the RTI process, the teachers and administration decided it would be advantageous to try an in-class therapy approach for all students receiving speech and language services. The psychologist was also asked to visit the students in the classroom. Small group roundtable discussions provided the perfect avenue for the SLP and psychologist to provide intervention to the identified students as well as others whom the teacher thought might benefit. Students were more responsive and consistent in therapy because they were not being singled out by leaving the classroom or by being the only ones receiving the interventions. The psychologist was able to model appropriate conflict resolution strategies as situations presented themselves in the roundtable setting.

High School

A student at a grade 9-12 school was falling behind in his class work, and as a result, his grades were falling. The school had just begun to implement the RTI process and had established a school-based team of professionals to review cases of individual students who were not making adequate progress in the classroom. This student, in addition to falling behind with his grades, had also scored below the benchmark on the most recent literacy screening assessment. This student's situation was discussed at the school-based team meeting. It was noted that his grades had fallen behind in all areas. The team decided to contact the mother. The mother reported that there were no unusual circumstances at home. The team decided to give this student extra help in the classroom on paragraph summarization strategies since the teachers noticed his falling grades were related to unfinished reading assignments which resulted in unanswered questions. After about 6 weeks of effective strategy instruction, this students' grades rose back to previous levels and his next screening assessment scores reflected above the benchmark performance.

Resources

Articles and information: Models of RTI across the nation including: Arizona Colorado Oregon Washington Wisconsin	Arizona RTI: Response to Intervention http://www.arizonarti.net/ Colorado Department of Education http://www.cde.state.co.us/cdesped/RTI.asp Oregon Department of Education http://www.ode.state.or.us/initiatives/idea/rti.aspx Office of Superintendent of Public Instruction – Washington http://www.k12.wa.us/SpecialEd/RTI.aspx Wisconsin Department of Public Instruction http://www.dpi.state.wi.us/sped/rti.html
Paper: *New Roles in Response to Intervention: Creating Success for Schools and Children.* National Association of School Psychologists This paper is a collaboration among associations that outlines the various roles that their professionals can play in the RTI process. The following associations are included: ASHA, DLD, IRA, LDA, NASP, NCLD, NEA, and SSWAA.	http://www.nasponline.org/advocacy/ New%20Roles%20in%20RTI.pdf or National Association of School Psychologists http://nasponline.org/
State Information: These state documents list a one-page basic description of each state's system of support for schools, including organizational structure, school support teams, and services provided to schools.	The Center for Comprehensive School Reform and Improvement http://www.centerforcsri.org/pubs/StateSystemSupport Profiles.pdf or The Center for Comprehensive School Reform and Improvement http://www.centerforcsri.org/

References

Fuchs, D. & Fuchs, L. S. (2006) Introduction to Response to Intervention: What, why, and how valid is it? *Reading Research Quarterly, 41*(1), 93-99.

Fuchs, D., Fuchs, L. S., & Compton, D. L. (2004). Identifying reading disabilities by responsiveness-to-instruction: Specifying measures and criteria. *Learning Disability Quarterly, 27*(4), 216-227.

Ikeda, M. J., Tilly, W. D., Stumme, J., Volmer, L., & Allison, R. (1996). Agency-wide implementation of problem solving consultation: Foundations, current implementation, and future directions. *School Psychology Quarterly, 11*(3), 228-243.

Reflection

Answer these questions to gauge your familiarity with the variety of RTI approaches.

1. Are you hearing more and more about a tiered process to helping students learn through your state, district, county, or building-level meetings?

    ❏ Yes   ❏ No   ❏ Haven't Noticed

2. Are you discussing with central office personnel, peers, other administrators, or teachers aspects of helping students learn though differentiated instruction?

    ❏ Yes   ❏ No   ❏ Haven't Noticed

3. Are you noticing an increasing number of articles in professional publications or on professional association Web sites about successful RTI programs across the country?

    ❏ Yes   ❏ No   ❏ Haven't Noticed

4. With which tiered approach(es) are you most familiar?

    _____

    _____

    _____

    _____

    _____

    _____

    _____

    _____

    _____

    _____

    _____

    _____

    _____

    _____

    _____

    _____

Part 2

Launching an RTI Initiative at Your School

> **Advance Organizer**
>
> You know basic information about RTI: What it is, what it is not, purposes, legal roots, and development. In this section you will find answers to the following questions:
>
> - Why launch an RTI initiative?
> - What building blocks do you already have in place?
> - What components should you address?
> - How might you proceed?

Before we discuss launching an RTI initiative, let's consider the word "initiative." We have made the point in Part 1 that RTI is not another new "thing." Therefore, we do not want the term "initiative" to convey that idea. We use "initiative" to mean a concerted effort to provide a systematic approach that falls within the boundaries of what is now called "Response to Intervention." If you are thinking of launching an RTI initiative, we interpret that to mean that, despite what you have been doing to meet the needs of the students in your school to date, you are thinking about becoming more deliberate and organized about your approach to put in place practices that are associated with RTI.

Chapter 4:

Why Launch an RTI Initiative?

▽ **Rationale**
▽ **Scenarios**
▽ **Resources**
▽ **Reflection**

As a school leader, you have a lot on your plate. You certainly don't need to begin new initiatives, or refine those in progress unless there is good reason. There may be several good reasons for you to consider beginning an RTI initiative at your school, some with an internal impetus and some with an external one. See if any of the reasons below resonate with you. There are, of course, other reasons.

Rationale

Parents at your school are beginning to inquire about RTI.

Information on the Internet is widely accessible to parents; more and more Web resources are available for RTI. The word is getting out about the value of RTI in addressing students' needs across a range of problems. The idea of providing assistance to students who may be struggling for a variety of reasons without their having to fail academically or meet special education eligibility criteria to obtain the help they need resonates with parents. Understandably, parents of children and adolescents who are having academic or behavior problems would be very interested in your school's offering options for them.

You are hearing about RTI in many professional circles and like to be on the cutting edge.

Are you hearing about RTI at the professional meetings you attend or reading about it in professional publications? You may like what you have learned about RTI and think that it will help your school take the next step in going from good to great. Certainly the desire for continuous improvement provides a cogent rationale for proceeding with an RTI initiative. A word of caution, however, is the need to focus school improvement efforts so that you don't have too many initiatives going at once. We will develop this idea later in this part.

You know it is not right to label students as having disabilities when their academic or behavior difficulties can be resolved with less drastic measures.

Federal mandates to serve students with disabilities can shape the way schools think about struggling students. In their eagerness to help students who are having learning problems, schools have looked to special education as a resource. While this direction is appropriate for perhaps 15% of the population, it is not the answer for all students who struggle academically or behaviorally. The simple reason is that not all these students have disabilities. They may need stronger basic instruction or more additional assistance than is typically available in general education. Labeling such students as having learning disabilities or behavioral disorders to provide the assistance they need poses an ethical dilemma. In an RTI approach, a school has mechanisms for providing needed help for teachers and students so that special education is not the only option, with special education remaining as an option for those who truly have disabilities.

You want all your students to succeed; you are not happy with your achievement data and you are concerned with meeting Adequate Yearly Progress.

At the heart of the mission of every school is the desire for all students to be successful. When individual students or groups of students struggle to meet state standards, schools are challenged to create systems to address the problem. Whatever professional, ethical, or moral purpose may have motivated concern for student achievement in the past, schools are now faced with the added pressure of NCLB accountability requirements. NCLB requires schools to make Adequate Yearly Progress (AYP) for all public elementary school and secondary school students, as well as for specific subgroups. These subgroups identified by NCLB include economically disadvantaged students, students from major racial and ethnic groups, students with disabilities, and students with limited English proficiency. Serious consequences accompany failure to meet AYP requirements. An RTI initiative can provide a systematic approach to meeting the learning needs of **all** students.

Your district or state expects you to initiate this process.

Many states and districts are somewhere along the continuum of designing RTI initiatives and implementing them. If it is clear that this is a direction your district has embraced, then you need to proceed accordingly. You may not have a choice. Although this perhaps is not the most palatable reason for launching an RTI initiative, it may be your reality. Take heart, it really is a good idea!

Scenarios

Elementary School

A K-5 school has 15% of their students being identified as students with learning disabilities. The principal has been concerned about this incidence and starts to think that this may be too high. (She's right; 5% to 6% would be more in line with national prevalence figures.) She plans to launch an RTI initiative to address other options for meeting students' academic needs.

Middle School

The grade chairs of a 6-8 school have made the principal aware of a serious problem. Several teachers are having discipline problems in their classrooms that are seriously interfering with learning. The principal knows that he needs to sort out these problems in terms of those that can be ameliorated at the classroom level with better (or different) classroom management approaches and those for which individual student behavior plans may be warranted. The principal reasons that putting an RTI system in place will help with this sorting process.

High School
The principal of an inner-city high school has many students who are reading at a fourth-grade level or below, and who are struggling mightily in their academic classes. Several of these students have previously been referred for possible placement in special education and have not qualified. The principal wants to explore an RTI approach that will help these students improve their reading and meet academic standards.

Resources

Article:	Prasse, D. (n.d.) *Why adopt an RTI model?*
Article explaining the purposes of establishing RTI	Washington, DC: RTI Action Network. http://www.rtinetwork.org/Learn/Why/ar/WhyRTI

Reflection

Take the time to think about why you might want to launch an RTI initiative, because your rationale may affect how you approach the process.

My rationale for considering an RTI approach:

_____

_____

_____

_____

_____

_____

_____

_____

_____

_____

_____

_____

_____

_____

_____

_____

_____

_____

_____

_____

_____

_____

Chapter 5:

What Building Blocks Do You Already Have in Place?

∇ **Practices**
∇ **Beliefs**
∇ **Scenarios**
∇ **Resources**
∇ **References**
∇ **Reflection**

It is very likely that beginning an RTI initiative will not mean that you are starting from scratch.

You may have several building blocks already in place that will serve as a foundation. Think of RTI as a framework for integrating the good things you are doing to meet students' needs and for guiding improvement efforts. Taking stock in your current status provides cues for start up and helps you to feel that RTI is doable. Looking at the practices you currently employ and the beliefs upon which your educational approach is based helps set the stage for an RTI approach.

Practices

Teachers use sound instruction.

If teachers have been working to identify and utilize scientifically based instruction, you have an important piece in place. With NCLB came the focus on evidence-based practice that calls for careful selection of programs/techniques based on evidence that they work. For teachers to provide sound instruction, they must implement the practice the way it was intended—with fidelity. Another aspect of sound instruction is that teachers differentiate instruction for the diverse learners in today's schools.

> To differentiate instruction is to recognize students' varying background knowledge, readiness, language, preferences in learning, interests, and to react responsively. Differentiated instruction is a process to approach teaching and learning for students of differing abilities in the same class. The intent of differentiating instruction is to maximize each student's growth and individual success by meeting each student where he or she is, and assisting in the learning process. (Hall, 2002, p. 1)

In general, teachers who differentiate instruction employ a variety of practices other than the whole-class lecture method and consider student strengths and learning challenges in work students do. For example, teachers may use flexible grouping in teaching and provide options in assignments.

Fidelity of scientifically based methods is ensured.

As we mentioned in the previous section, part of providing sound instruction is to make sure that the scientifically based instruction is carried out the way it was designed. Selecting scientifically based instructional practices is only the first step. Teachers then have to implement those practices the way the researchers did when they tested them. Only when they carry them out faithfully, adhering to the same principles that were used in the validation research, can we assert that they are using scientifically based instruction. Having a strong program of ongoing professional development is the beginning of ensuring fidelity of scientifically based methods. It may include a component in which instructional coaches work directly with teachers to ensure fidelity. Principals also need a monitoring system. For example, you might conduct walk-throughs of classrooms where you ascertain that instruction is being carried out appropriately.

Options are offered to meet learning needs.

Despite a focus on good classroom instruction and well-managed classrooms you will likely have students who need more than the classroom teacher can give. There will be some students who have academic or behavioral challenges that you will have to address with additional resources. If you have some supports in place for these students, that's a start. Your goal would be to offer a variety of services in varying degrees of intensity to address learning needs, but some options may already be in place. For example, you may have a reading specialist or Title 1 teacher who provides additional support to students not reading up to grade level. You may have special programs before or after school to support mastery of standards. If you are at a secondary school you might have intensive reading classes for students reading below a certain level. However you may structure your options, if you provide more than just the special education services that are required by law and students can have assistance in a number of ways outside of special education, you have an important building block upon which to develop a systematic approach to addressing all students' needs.

A committee or team coordinates supports.

Most schools have a "child study" type team to address concerns about students who are struggling academically or behaviorally. However, it is common for the group to manage the referral process for special education services and to think of themselves as the stepping-stone to special education. On the other hand, some schools have a group of people who routinely meet to solve problems of student performance who do not perceive their function to be a special education referral chute. The idea is to have a system in place to address student's learning difficulties in which efforts are coordinated across the school for students who underachieve for a variety of reasons. You have a leg up in this area if you have a systematic way to address diverse learning needs across the school and do not have different groups designated to handle specific services.

A data management system exists.

With accountability standards set by NCLB, schools usually collect a lot of data. However, unless a school has a system in place to manage the data, it may not be used to the best advantage. Data has to be organized, stored, and retrieved in a way that makes the information accessible to teachers and support staff. For example, you might have a computer program that processes data and is user friendly, as well as a team that reviews data on a regular basis.

Data are used to inform instruction and service delivery.

Using data is a challenge in many schools. It would be a tremendous advantage if the faculty were accustomed to analyzing data and applying results to improve classroom instruction and make decisions about support services. If this were common practice at your school, classroom instruction would change as a result of data analysis, and programs or classes would be structured to meet the needs found in assessment. Further, participation in any special programs or services for struggling students would be based on assessment results. For example, in addition to the required state or district assessment you might gather literacy data on at least a semester basis for students experiencing reading difficulty. (This frequency may not be sufficient for some students but it's a start.) Teachers would either adjust their classroom instruction based on the data or obtain other supports for their students not making sufficient progress. You might also have a group who review high-stakes assessment data on a regular basis and determine what other data are needed on struggling students. For example, your group might discover that 20% of your students are reading below grade level. However, the available data do not pinpoint the problem. So they might recommend that more in-depth reading assessment be done to identify whether students are having decoding, fluency, vocabulary, or other comprehension problems.

Teachers, support personnel, and administrators work together to meet the learning needs of all students.

Schools where collaboration exists across grades and subjects, among general and special education teachers, among teachers and support personnel, and where principals take an active leadership role to facilitate this work are in an advantageous position to launch an RTI initiative. It would be difficult to engage in processes required for an RTI initiative if a school did not have a culture supporting collaborative efforts. All educators in a building have to assume responsibility for educating all of the students within that building. However, it takes more than a supportive culture; infrastructures have to be in place to permit teachers to work together. In some schools this translates into administrators building a schedule that accommodates teachers' meeting together. Some schools have a teacher leadership team with broad representation with whom the principal works closely to address school improvement efforts.

Teachers and administrators participate in ongoing professional development.

There will be new things for everyone to learn in launching an RTI initiative. If your school culture already supports ongoing professional development, where teachers and administrators think of professional development as an integral tool for school improvement, that is a huge plus. Of course they also have to actively engage in relevant activities. For example, a principal may recognize that teachers need more than just a workshop on content literacy to help students improve in comprehension of textbook material. She might employ a reading coach to support teachers' implementation of what they have learned in this area. The litmus test for effective professional development at a school is that there is a high participation rate, teachers actually implement what they learn, and it has a positive impact on student outcomes.

Beliefs

All students can learn.

Unless teachers have an optimistic view that they can be successful in facilitating student learning for all students, some students will be left behind. Teachers have to demonstrate this belief by having high expectations for ALL students and assisting each student to meet requirements. This belief includes not giving up on groups of students by thinking in stereotypes (e.g., "THOSE kids are not interested in learning").

What educators who believe this might say:	*What educators who believe this would NOT say:*
I need to find out why Scott is not learning in my class.	Scott is lazy.
I should meet the special education teacher who works with Veronica to find out how to help her learn in my class.	Veronica has a learning disability; I don't expect her to meet the standards of this grade/subject.

In learning, one size does not fit all.

In order to implement differentiated instruction and plan for additional instructional supports, the faculty has to value diversity in approaches. First, teachers have to be grounded in the understanding that differences exist among students in several areas: ethnicity, linguistics, ability, learning style, interests, and motivation. They have to be motivated by the belief that it is their professional responsibility to address those differences to maximize student learning.

What educators who believe this might say:	*What educators who believe this would NOT say:*
Leroy has trouble reading his social studies text. I am finding other resources to help him understand social studies material so that his learning is not dependent on reading the text.	Leroy can't read the textbook; that's why he is failing social studies.
When I plan for the week, I think of alternative assignments for Maria to stretch her application of learning.	Maria is by far the brightest student in my class. She gets bored with the work I give the class.

Waiting for students to fail is not a good approach.

As the saying goes, "An ounce of prevention is worth a pound of cure." However, some of our structures within education have been built on a wait-to-fail model. Such is the case when, for example, we wait until third grade to attend to students who are not learning to read the way we would expect, or we transition eighth-graders to high school without attending to reading deficiencies. Teachers must be committed to prevention of school failure and appreciate the role of early intervening in situations where students are struggling. This is as important at the secondary level as it is at the elementary level.

What educators who believe this might say:	*What educators who believe this would NOT say:*
We need to figure out why Lashondra is struggling now so that she can get the help she needs.	Lashondra is struggling in my class. Let's see how she does by the end of the semester.
Matthew is struggling in kindergarten with phonemic awareness. What program or technique might we use with him to help him learn in this area?	Matthew is only in kindergarten. Let's give him time to catch up with peers in learning phonemic awareness.

Research has value in guiding education.

Research has to be perceived by educators as a valuable companion to practice. It is not just for university professors or graduate students. Despite the fact that NCLB and IDEA 2004 require educators to rely on research for instructional methods, a research base for what educators do makes practical sense. Trial and error consumes valuable time that neither students nor teachers have to waste.

What educators who believe this might say:	*What educators who believe this would NOT say:*
I try to be a conscientious consumer of research and see if the methods and analyses make sense.	You can't believe what you read in research. Anybody can manipulate statistics to prove a point.
I think it makes sense to rely on proven methods and not waste time shooting from the hip.	Teachers don't need research; the school of hard knocks teaches you what you need to know about learning.

Assessment is crucial to instruction.

Teachers can be turned off to assessment if they feel that testing is a dead end and takes too much time away from instruction. Assuming a delicate balance is achieved between fruitful assessment and instruction, teachers have to appreciate the information that assessment results can give them to support their work in the classroom. Assessment can identify learning and behavior problems before they get out of hand and can provide information about the extent of progress made. Achievement in specific areas can be pinpointed so that educators know what to do to help students.

What educators who believe this might say:	*What educators who believe this would NOT say:*
I would like to see us select the tests we use wisely to get the information we need.	All testing is just a waste of time.
Results on the GRADE* indicate that Jackie is more than 2 years below in reading. I think she needs the help with reading that the intensive reading class provides.	I feel that Jackie should be in the intensive reading class.

* GRADE is the Group Reading Assessment and Diagnostic Evaluation (see Williams, 2001).

Education is a partnership.

The saying, "It takes a village to raise a child" has become cliché. However, the belief that no one educator can be successful meeting the learning challenges of the diverse students who walk through the classroom door is paramount to successful student outcomes. All faculty and administrators share the responsibility for student achievement. For example, it is not the special education teacher's job alone to teach students with disabilities. Because most students will spend time in the general education classroom, classroom teachers must also consider the education of these students as their job. Families have to be regarded as important partners in education and be integrally involved in the school. They must be central participants.

What educators who believe this might say:	What educators who believe this would NOT say:
The information Nicky's mother gave me about how she manages his behavior at home has been very valuable.	Nicky's mother is a real pest. She always wants to talk with me about his behavior at home and school.
I'm not at all sure how to deal with Pedro. He just arrived in this country and doesn't speak English. I will talk to the ESOL teacher to see if he has any pointers.	Pedro doesn't speak English. I can't do anything for him.

There is no quick fix.

Educators are often gripped by a sense of urgency to help students and turn around achievement problems quickly. That is understandable. Accountability standards reinforce that urgency. However, you and your staff have to recognize that intensive and sustained efforts are needed for substantive school improvement and that desired outcomes cannot be achieved overnight. (This is hard when your local newspaper publishes test results yearly!) If you and your staff recognize that this is a long-term process that will take time, you will likely direct your efforts in a positive direction. You won't be tempted to change abruptly to a different approach when you don't solve the problem immediately.

What educators who believe this might say:	What educators who believe this would NOT say:
We have been using differentiated instruction for a year now across the school. We still have too many students who are having difficulty in core instruction. Let's make sure we are using sound instruction with fidelity and are using support resources appropriately to enhance core instruction.	We have been using differentiated instruction for a year now across the school. We still have too many students who are having difficulty in their core instruction. Let's try something new.
It takes time for teachers to adopt new approaches. We will support implementation of our schoolwide literacy approach with instructional coaching.	We can't get all our teachers on board with our schoolwide literacy approach so we might as well give up.

The system will change only if I change.

Change is difficult for everyone. It is easy to think about a system needing to change without taking to heart the need to change personally. This notion requires accepting personal responsibility for school improvement.

What educators who believe this might say:	What educators who believe this would NOT say:
I will pay close attention to early signs of struggle in my classroom.	This school has to pay more attention to kids who fall through the cracks.
I might have to think of other ways to teach science because many of my students aren't meeting science standards.	I always cover the textbook when I teach science.

Scenarios

Elementary School

A Title 1 elementary school has been going about the business of school reform seriously for a number of years. Many of their challenges have revolved around working with children in a high-poverty neighborhood. The principal takes inventory of the building blocks discussed above and notes that he has many in place. The two that stand out as missing are "Fidelity of scientifically based methods is ensured" and "A committee or team coordinates supports." Regarding the first one, he has a reading coach who works with teachers to implement the Open Court reading program they are using. However, he realizes that he doesn't have a system to monitor implementation. The other missing piece relates to the process in place to address students who are struggling. The school has a child study team that handles referrals to special education and another team who addresses the needs of English Language Learners (ELL). There is no other group that meets to discuss issues related to students meeting standards. They do have some supports in place; for example, the Title 1 teacher works with small groups of students to supplement reading and math instruction. However, there is no committee that deliberates on the problems of students unless they are being referred to special education or they are ELL. Further, these committees work separately. As he reviews the beliefs upon which RTI rests, he feels confident that the culture of his school is rooted in them.

Middle School

An upper-middle class, suburban neighborhood has a middle school where most students are meeting state standards. However, they have students who are not, including students with disabilities. Also, they think that some of the students who are meeting standards could be doing better. The principal thinks about the building blocks of RTI and notes that "Teachers, support personnel, and administrators work together to meet the learning needs of all students" could use some strengthening. He feels that the teachers really do not take ownership of the students with disabilities in their classes. They look too much to the special education teachers to meet the needs of "their" students. He wonders if the resource classes in special education, which are together in portable classrooms outside the building, might contribute to this separateness. He also suspects that at the root of this practice might be that they do not believe "All students can learn," contributing to a lowering of expectations for the students with disabilities in the general education classes. Regarding the students who could be doing better but who are meeting state standards, he suspects that the "In learning, one size does not fit all" belief may not be firmly planted in teachers' value systems and, therefore, they may not be differentiating instruction. They may be teaching to average students and not sufficiently challenging higher achieving students. Therefore, "Teachers use sound instruction" needs attention.

High School

The principal of a high school has been hearing about RTI, but mostly about what is being done at the elementary schools in her district. It seems a little overwhelming to think about putting an RTI system in place at her school. The size alone makes any change difficult. However, when she thinks about attending to building blocks, she starts to feel a little better about taking on the challenge of an RTI initiative. Specifically, faculty and administrators have been implementing a professional learning community (PLC)* approach to professional development to tackle the many issues involved in meeting the needs of a large, diverse group of adolescents. So she knows that "Teachers and administrators participate in ongoing professional development" is a building block that will serve her school well in contemplating an RTI initiative. She thinks that this structure will provide a framework within which to look at other practices, like "Data are used to inform instruction and service delivery" and "Options are offered to meet learning needs." The teacher leaders who are spearheading the PLC approach are good "go-to" people to discuss what an RTI initiative might do for the high school and to work with her in planning and implementation.

*For additional information about PLCs see:

DuFour, R., & Eaker, R. (1998). *Professional learning communities at work: Best practices for enhancing student achievement.* Bloomington, IN: National Educational Service; Alexandria, VA: ASCD.

Tucker, C. (2008). *Implementing and sustaining professional learning communities in support of student learning.* Alexandria, VA: Educational Research Service.

Resources

Belief Survey: A 26-item survey to identify beliefs of administrators, teachers and support personnel that are foundational to RTI	Batsche, G. (n.d.). *Beliefs Survey.* Florida Problem Solving/Response to Intervention Project http://www.rtinetwork.org/images/stories/Downloads/beliefs.pdf
Informational Survey: A 16-item survey to obtain information about teachers' skill levels in assessment and instruction/intervention practices fundamental to RTI	Batsche, G. (n.d.). *Perceptions of RtI Skills Survey.* Florida Problem Solving/Response to Intervention Project. http://www.rtinetwork.org/images/stories/Downloads/perceptionsofrtiskills.pdf

References

Hall, T. (2002). *Differentiated instruction.* Wakefield, MA: National Center on Accessing the General Curriculum. Retrieved June 21, 2008, from http://www.cast.org/publications/ncac/ncac_diffinstruc.html

Williams, K. T. (2001). *Group Reading Assessment and Diagnostic Evaluation (GRADE).* Circle Pines, MN: American Guidance Service.

Reflection

Gauging where you are with building blocks of RTI will help you move forward to implement an initiative. The "Taking Stock of Building Blocks" forms on the following pages will help you assess status of practices and beliefs. You can have individuals or groups complete the forms. At a minimum you should seek input from other administrators in your building, teachers across grade or subject areas—including general and special educators, as well as the reading specialist, reading coach, counselor, school psychologist, and speech-language pathologist. We suggest that you gather a group of school leaders from among those just named to discuss results of the inquiry. You might also find the resources listed above useful in your inquiry and discussion.

Taking Stock of RTI Building Blocks – Practices

Place a check mark along the line in each cell indicating the degree to which the practice is employed.

	To a Great Degree	*Not at All*
Teachers use sound instruction.		
	Notes:	
Fidelity of scientifically based methods is ensured.		
	Notes:	
Options are offered to meet learning needs.		
	Notes:	
A committee or team coordinates supports.		
	Notes:	
A data management system exists.		
	Notes:	
Data are used to inform instruction and service delivery.		
	Notes:	
Teachers, support personnel, and administrators work together to meet the learning needs of all our students.		
	Notes:	
Teachers and administrators participate in ongoing professional development.		
	Notes:	

Persons completing the form: _____

Ehren, B. J., Ehren, T. C., & Proly, J. L. (2009) *Response to Intervention: An action guide for school leaders*. Alexandria, VA. Educational Research Service.

May be reproduced.

Taking Stock of RTI Building Blocks – Beliefs

Place a check mark along the line in each cell indicating the degree to which the belief is evident.

	To a Great Degree	*Not at All*
All students can learn.		
	Notes:	
In learning, one size does not fit all.		
	Notes:	
Waiting for students to fail is not a good approach.		
	Notes:	
Research has a value in guiding education.		
	Notes:	
Assessment is crucial to instruction.		
	Notes:	
Education is a partnership.		
	Notes:	
There is no quick fix.		
	Notes:	
The system will change only if I change.		
	Notes:	

Persons completing the form: _____

Ehren, B. J., Ehren, T. C., & Proly, J. L. (2009) *Response to Intervention: An action guide for school leaders*. Alexandria, VA. Educational Research Service.

Chapter 6:

What Components Should You Address?

∇ **Components**
∇ **Scenarios**
∇ **Resources**
∇ **References**
∇ **Reflection**

You know from reading Part 1 that a number of RTI iterations exist. However there are some elements that most people would agree are necessary for an RTI approach. These include establishing a focus, employing high-quality instruction/intervention, building a tiered system of instruction/intervention, creating a system for data-based decision making, developing infrastructures to support implementation, and facilitating the change process. We will discuss what these components entail here, and later we will deal with steps for implementation when we address the last question, "How might you proceed?" (*Note: In the **Reflection** section there is a form (page 73) to capture questions you have about the components described and to record the answers you find in the additional resources listed. Instead of waiting to use this form, you may want to keep it handy as you are reading this section to jot down questions as you read.*)

Components

Establishing a Focus

You will have to decide what kind of an approach you will develop, depending on your school's priorities or what your state or district requires. Although there are different orientations to RTI, all are rooted in a focus on student outcomes.

Orientation

As outlined in Part 1, many approaches address *literacy* acquisition specifically. Others take a *general problem-solving* approach with academic achievement and behavior as targets. In general, problem-solving iterations follow some variation of the following process (Graner, Faggella-Luby, & Fritschmann, 2005):

Step 1: *Problem identification*—Define the problem in observable terms. Report rate, intensity, and duration of the problem.

Step 2: *Problem analysis and intervention design*—Validate the existence of the problem and identify appropriate instruction considering individual student strengths and challenges.

Step 3: *Implementation and evaluation of the intervention*—Provide intervention, monitor the student's progress, and ensure fidelity of implementation of the intervention.

More recently a few iterations focus on *math*. Your decision should be consistent with state and district policy, should be based on the priorities established in your school improvement plan, and should reflect the needs of the students in your community. The danger with studying other schools' versions of RTI is that you may select one to emulate that does not make sense for your students and your community.

A frequently neglected aspect of RTI is its use in determination of eligibility for special education. Although it is likely that district and state regulations will have an impact on your use of RTI for this purpose, this aspect of RTI should at least be on your radar screen. The following position on RTI was expressed by the National Joint Committee for Learning Disabilities (NJCLD), a coalition of many member organizations concerned with special education or learning disabilities:

> In addition to the preventive and remedial services this approach may provide to at-risk students, it shows promise for contributing data useful for identifying LD. Thus, a student exhibiting (1) significantly low achievement and (2) insufficient RTI may be regarded as being at risk for LD and, in turn, as possibly in need of special education and related services. The assumption behind this paradigm, which has been referred to as a dual discrepancy (L. S. Fuchs, Fuchs, & Speece, 2002), is that when provided with quality instruction and remedial services, a student without disabilities will make satisfactory progress. (National Joint Committee on Learning Disabilities, 2005, p. 1)

Student Outcomes

Whatever the focus of your initiative, the target is improved student outcomes at your school. That target provides the guiding force for your RTI development and implementation. For example, if your school has serious problems with student behavior, then you would be remiss to exclude a problem-solving behavioral approach in your iteration. If literacy achievement were an issue, you would want to be sure to deal specifically with literacy. One does not have to be the focus to the exclusion of the other. You should decide on a focus that will improve the achievement of standards by your students.

Things to consider:

1. Check the Web sites of your state department of education and district to ascertain how they define RTI.

2. Make the links to your school improvement plan clear. RTI should not be an entity detached from your overall approach to school improvement.

3. Arrive at your decision with stakeholders. Launching an RTI initiative will take time and effort. The buy-in of teachers, administrators, and parents is crucial to its success.

4. All educators and parents should be able to explain the school's approach to RTI, as well as the rationale for it. Everyone should be on the same page with regard to what you are doing.

Employing High-Quality Instruction/Intervention

The instructional practices of teachers must be of high quality. This means, as we have discussed previously and you have probably heard repeated in many venues, that core instruction and intervention must be based on research.

Core Instruction

High-quality core instruction is the linchpin of RTI. It includes scientifically based instruction with differentiation for the variety of learners in the classroom. Unless you can be sure that teachers are using proven practices to enable students to master core curriculum, and are taking into consideration differences in student learning, you won't know if some students really need additional support. It is not efficient to allocate resources to supplementary kinds of programs and services in instances where the problem can be addressed by improving instruction in the core curriculum.

Intervention

It is also essential that when supplementary services are offered, they too be based on research. Teachers and support personnel working with students in more intensive services (intervention) should use proven methods. Additional services can be costly; you do not want to squander resources on ineffective practices.

Fidelity of Implementation

An important consideration is that you cannot judge whether students are responding positively to instruction and intervention if you are unsure of the nature of what students are receiving. The fidelity principle requires that teachers have a thorough understanding of the methods or program they are implementing. This is a professional development issue. They will need more than a single workshop to make this happen. They will need support during implementation. Having an instructional coaching component is an excellent way to provide this support. Closely tied to fidelity is "dosage." Not only must teachers implement instruction/intervention the way it was designed; they also need to do so with the frequency and duration that research indicates are needed. George Batsche (n.d.) recommended the use of an intervention log to document three aspects of intervention integrity: the time (each day) that the student received the intervention, the program or strategy selected for the intervention, and the focus of the intervention.

As an administrator your bottom line is monitoring fidelity. You will need a procedure to ensure fidelity of implementation of instruction/intervention. The common practice of walk-throughs can help in this regard. However, the question is whether you can really ascertain what you need to know about fidelity from a brief encounter like a walk-through. Below is an example of an amended walk-through procedure in which the principal asks probing questions to obtain information that cannot be observed in a limited sample of classroom teaching. In this format, the key elements the principal is looking for are listed in the first column, the evidence is noted in the second column, and the third column lists probing questions that can uncover more in-depth information than can be observed in a short time period. The example is for implementation of Content Enhancement Routines for enhancing content teaching validated by research at the University of Kansas Center for Research on Learning (KUCRL).

Table 6.1. Example—Content Enhancement Routines (CER) Walk-Through Guide		
Key Elements	**Evidence**	**Probing Questions**
Content Enhancement Routines are being used consistently in instruction.	Information written on board Posters of devices	How many times have you used the _____ routine? With what classes?
"Cue, Do, Review" sequence is employed.	Student folders/notebooks with devices	What kind of things do you say when you cue students during CER instruction? How do you review information with a CER visual device?
	Teacher's lesson plans (Ask for copies of draft devices and final co-constructed versions. They should be different.)	
Device is co-constructed with students.		What kind of input did students give when you were constructing the device with them?
	Classroom instruction	
Teacher works from a draft of the device.		Did colleagues provide input regarding your draft device?
Teacher fosters students' connections among ideas using the device.		How do you use the device to help students make connections with the topic content?

Things to consider:

1. Carefully investigate the research base of programs or techniques you are considering (see resources at the end of this chapter). Ask to see the research upon which a program or technique is based.

2. Make sure teachers' instruction is rooted in standards, in addition to being scientifically based.

3. Beware of vendors labeling products as "RTI" products. If you think of RTI as a framework, there are no RTI products *per se*; rather there are scientifically based programs or techniques that may be utilized within an RTI framework.

Building a Tiered System of Instruction/Intervention

Even with the highest-quality instruction in general education classrooms, there will be students whose academic achievement or behavior will need intervention. It is essential to RTI that options are available for students who need more than differentiated instruction in the general education classroom.

Tiers

In RTI, services and interventions are provided to struggling learners at increasing levels of intensity based on performance data. It doesn't matter how many tiers or levels your district defines in its framework, nor if they even label the continuum "tiers." What matters is that a systematic approach is in place to deliver the core instruction and any additional intervention necessary to help students succeed.

Intervention is not a single program, but rather an array of options that may ultimately include special education services at the end of the continuum. A key is to have options outside of special education that increase in intensity and are selected based on student need. The basic notion is that students who are "nonresponders" to high-quality instruction in general education would receive additional help in the next tier, and those who do not respond by making sufficient progress in that tier would go on to the next.

The most common structure is the three-tiered version that may be called by different names and may involve different activities within tiers. Johnson, Mellard, Fuchs, and McKnight (2006) refer to primary, secondary, and tertiary intervention. (We'll call Tier 1 "Primary Instruction.") In this schema, Tier 1 includes primary supports for students in the general education classroom. Tier 2 consists of secondary interventions in specialized groups for at-risk students. Tier 3 involves specialized individualized systems for students with intensive needs which may include "specially designed instruction" in special education. Here is an example:

Universal Instruction (Tier 1)—Primary Instruction

- Evidence-based practices implemented by classroom teachers
- Differentiated instruction
- Screening
- Frequent progress monitoring (a.k.a., formative assessment)

Targeted Interventions (Tier 2)—Secondary Intervention

- Interventions designed to address specific needs identified through screening and progress monitoring
- Interventions supplement universal instruction rather than supplant it

- Academic interventions typically delivered in small groups that may be a standard treatment protocol (e.g., the Lindamood Phoneme Sequencing Program for Reading, Spelling, and Speech [LiPS] or different interventions designed within the context of a problem-solving model)
- Progress monitoring continues

Specialized Treatments (Tier 3)—Tertiary Intervention

- Treatments designed to address limited progress in areas of targeted intervention
- Treatments delivered in small groups or individually
- Progress monitoring continues
- May be within general education or in special education (In some tiered models, special education would be considered Tier 4)

Integration and Movement

Whatever the number of tiers, they do not exist as isolated entities. The RTI framework provides a structure within which to establish a well-integrated system across general, compensatory, and special education. It is a golden opportunity to deconstruct the silos that often exist in schools with programs and processes and to create a unitary system for addressing student needs. The objective is that students receive what they need, when they need it. Tiers should not constitute a lock-step sequence that students have to follow to receive the help they need. For example (and this is important) a student who is already known to have a disability should not have to pass through Tier 2 before he receives the specially designed instruction he needs as part of special education.

Balance

It is important to strike a balance in the development and implementation of tiers. So, in a three-tier approach, we would want to pay significant attention to Tier 1 because the success of the majority of students will depend on it. A rule of thumb to consider is that between 80% and 90% of the students in your school should be successful with high-quality core instruction. As an outside figure, if you have more than 20% of your students having difficulty meeting standards, then you know that your core instruction needs attention. However, that will still leave another 10% to 15% who will need more intense services in Tier 2. Considering that, in a school of 500 students, between 50 and 75 students would be expected to receive targeted interventions, that is not a trivial planning number. That leaves a small number of students (1-5%) who will need more tailored interventions, which would include students who are eligible for special education services. Although this might involve from 5 to 25 students in the same school of 500, the services in this tier are more resource-intensive.

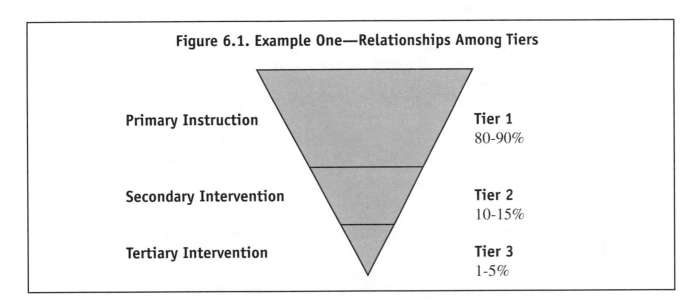

Figure 6.1. Example One—Relationships Among Tiers

Primary Instruction — Tier 1 — 80-90%

Secondary Intervention — Tier 2 — 10-15%

Tertiary Intervention — Tier 3 — 1-5%

A triangle is the most common graphic associated with a three-tier model (See Figure 6.1). However, we prefer the inverted triangle to make the statement that Tier 1 deserves our first consideration when launching an RTI initiative. This graphic depicts the proportion of students involved in the tiers; obviously the most students are served in Tier 1 and the fewest in Tier 3. The problem with this graphic is that it may be interpreted as a linear process, and it really is not. Students do not drop out of Tier 1 when they move to Tier 2. However, students may not be participating in Tier 2 if they are in Tier 3.

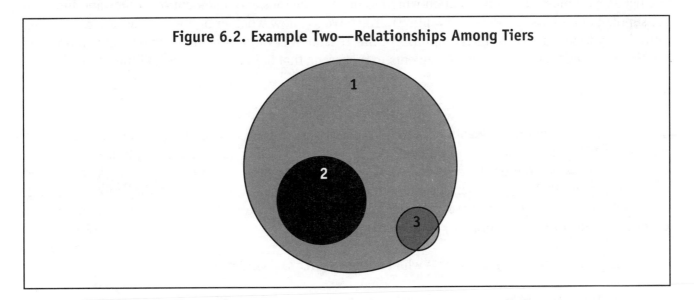

Figure 6.2. Example Two—Relationships Among Tiers

The circular depiction shows that Tier 2 and 3 take place within the context of Tier 1 (See Figure 6.2). This is meant to show that Tier 1 doesn't end when Tiers 2 or 3 are initiated. You will notice that a small part of Tier 3 falls outside of Tier 1, which is meant to signify the very small percentage of students in special education who are not in general education. This would only apply in approaches where special education is considered as part of Tier 3.

Things to consider:

1. If your state or district has defined an RTI framework, ascertain how many tiers they incorporate, how they define tiers, the activities they include in each tier, and where special education services fit into the framework.

2. Find out how your state or district is addressing the change in federal law that no longer requires a discrepancy formula for identifying students as having learning disabilities.

3. Establish how your state integrates data collected during progress monitoring in considering eligibility for special education and where other evaluation processes fit into the scheme.

4. If you utilize a *standard treatment protocol* for Tier 2, make sure you know the conditions under which the method worked: the number of minutes a day, number of days a week, and number of weeks to remediate the problem.

Creating a System of Data-Based Decision Making

When you design a system for providing increasingly intensive options for addressing students' learning needs, you must have a basis upon which to make decisions about student outcomes and the need for supplementary instruction (intervention). You have to know whether or not students are responding sufficiently to instruction or intervention. For this reason, RTI initiatives hinge on data generation and application. There are a number of elements in this arena that help to define an RTI initiative.

Universal Screening

The way schools identify students in need of Tier 2 intervention is to conduct screenings. Students who score below a certain prescribed point on the screening either receive intervention immediately or their progress is monitored for several weeks. In the latter case, students' growth rates are tracked to see if they are making sufficient progress in their classrooms. If they are not, they move to Tier 2. Some schools conduct screening several times during the year and others only once. The following are criteria for selecting a screening measure (Jenkins, 2003):

1. It needs to identify students who require further assessment.

2. It needs to be practical.

3. It needs to generate positive outcomes (accurately identifies students without consuming resources that could be put to better use).

An example of a screening tool used by schools to check students' literacy status is the Dynamic Indicators of Basic Early Literacy Skills (DIBELS) (n.d.), a set of standardized, individually administered measures of 1-minute measures.

Progress Monitoring

Progress monitoring is the process of assessing students' academic performance or behavior on a regular basis to evaluate the effectiveness of instruction and intervention. It has three purposes (National Center on Student Progress Monitoring, n.d.):

1. To determine whether children are profiting appropriately from the instructional program;

2. To build more effective programs for students who do not benefit; and

3. To estimate rates of student improvement.

It can be implemented with individual students or an entire class. Students' current levels of performance are determined and goals are identified for learning that will take place over time. The student's academic performance is measured on a weekly or monthly basis. Progress toward meeting the student's goals is measured by comparing expected and actual rates of learning. Based on these measurements, teaching is adjusted as needed. Typically the more intense the intervention, the more frequent the measures taken. Visual displays of data, such as charts, are used to depict learning trajectories and make decisions about changes within a tier or movement across a tier. A tool frequently used in academic programs is Curriculum-Based Measurement (CBM) to assess skills for progress monitoring such as math, reading, writing, and spelling. Each CBM test assesses all the different skills taught annually in the curriculum in exactly the same way but with different items. In this way scores attained at different times during the school year can be compared. As an example of CBM, a child may read aloud for 1 minute with the teacher counting the correct and incorrect responses made. The scores are recorded on a graph and compared to expected performance. There is a strong empirical base for progress monitoring (Fuchs & Fuchs, n.d.). There are, however, other instruments and procedures for conducting this type of formative assessment.

Data Management

With the importance of assessment to an RTI approach it is essential that data be collected, stored, and retrieved in an efficient manner. Data that are not accessible to educators are useless. Computer resources are available to facilitate this process; for example: (1) *AIMSweb,* a Web-based data management and reporting system based on CBM includes universal screening and progress-monitoring data, and (2) Pearson Benchmark, another Web-based system helps districts to test, report, and analyze student achievement data by taking multiple measures of student performance against standards at any time throughout the school year.

The purpose of efficient data management is to have a basis upon which to make decisions about student progress to ascertain whether other actions are necessary. While computerized tools are helpful, you will still need people to manage the process. Especially important is designating a team of professionals with broad representation across the school to reflect on the data and make the decisions about instructional practices and movement across tiers. For example, if a student is not making progress in reading comprehension, the group may help the classroom teacher adjust her instruction or they may recommend Tier 2 services. If a student is already in Tier 2 and not making progress, a decision must be made about what to do. It is then up to individual teachers to use data to adjust their instruction or to the decision-making team to make a recommendation for intervention.

Things to consider:

1. Screening and progress measures should be appropriate to your school level. For example, screening may be defined differently in a high school than it is in an elementary school.

2. You have to set criteria for how much progress is sufficient to determine that a student is responsive to intervention.

3. You might consider employing a data coach to help with data analysis.

Developing Infrastructures to Support Implementation

The desire to implement RTI must be accompanied by structures to make it happen. We have already discussed some of the infrastructures needed for implementation; for example, a system for data management and a procedure for monitoring fidelity of implementation. There are others that are important to address.

Use of Resources

You will need to think about who is doing universal screenings, progress monitoring, and data management, as well as providing Tier 2 and Tier 3 interventions. Unless you have the ability to hire new staff, you will have to redeploy the staff you have. Using existing staff in different ways will involve reconceptualizing roles of professionals including classroom teachers, reading specialists, learning disabilities specialists, speech-language pathologists, educational audiologists, school psychologists, school social workers, school counselors, occupational therapists, physical therapists, and other specialized instructional support personnel (related/pupil services personnel). In 2006, 13 organizations collaborated in outlining new or expanded roles of their constituencies from among the professionals named above. They focused on the contributions of a variety of professionals to program design, collaboration, and service to individuals or groups of students in RTI. "When you have read all of these papers, you will note that each staff member in each school building who works with struggling students has a role to play" (Collaborative Project, 2006, Introduction).

An important point about utilizing the expertise of special education teachers, including learning disabilities specialists, who understand diagnostic prescriptive approaches, is that their involvement cannot shortchange students with IEPs. The services listed on IEPs must be provided. However, certain delivery models, like self-contained special education classes, may be restructured to permit more flexible implementation of intervention services.

For school psychologists, RTI requires a shift in assessment orientation from traditional, norm-referenced approaches to a more pragmatic approach focused on measuring changes in individual performance over time (National Association of School Psychologists, 2006, p. 3). They could become your resident experts in CBM or other formative assessments and have more of a role in problem solving and progress monitoring.

Speech-language pathologists (SLPs) have a unique set of contributions to make to RTI considering their expertise in the language bases of literacy and learning, experience with collaborative approaches to intervention, and an understanding of the use of student outcomes data when making instructional decisions. In order to use them wisely, you have to think beyond their roles with speech problems and think of their roles with language and literacy.

However, as you help professionals reconceptualize their roles, it is essential that you tend to the practical aspects of their workloads. For some professionals, like school psychologists and SLPs, it would be difficult to add RTI to what they have been doing. Rather, they will have to redefine their workloads to accommodate RTI activities. From the perspective of the professionals, they must be open to change, willing to adapt to different service delivery models, and willing to discuss their possible contributions. They may need a new or enhanced skill set for which preservice and inservice professional development is required. For example, the IRA (International Reading Association) noted the roles of reading specialists in the RTI process as teachers for students experiencing reading difficulties, as literacy or reading coaches, or as supervisors/coordinators of reading/literacy. They outlined the qualifications for fulfilling these roles: Previous teaching experience, Master's degree with concentration in reading education, a minimum of 24 graduate credit hours in reading, language arts, and related courses, and an additional 6 credit hours of supervised practicum experience.

Promoting Collaboration

RTI requires that teachers, support professionals, and administrators work together on implementation. Although a culture of collegiality is necessary to this process, it is not enough. Structures must be created to permit collaboration on activities that are part of RTI. For example: (1) Teachers of the same grade or subject need the time and opportunity to interact with each other to calibrate their use of scientifically based instruction and to support each other in differentiated instruction; and, (2) If you create a team that is responsible for monitoring progress of students and exploring options for meeting all students' needs, then team members will need to include those meetings as an essential part of their work schedules and not use a "catch as catch can" method that may involve canceling instruction or intervention with students.

Partnerships with families are crucial to the success of an RTI initiative. Families should understand the purpose of an RTI approach and the nature of your approach. More specifically, they should have up-to-date information on their child's involvement in RTI. Mechanisms to share screening and progress monitoring information with families should be created. They should understand that service in preliminary tiers is not meant to withhold special education services, if they are needed. Inform parents of their right to refer their child, at any time, for evaluation for special education services as stipulated in IDEA 2004. Provide written material on the criteria for determining eligibility for special education under IDEA 2004 and the role of RTI data in making learning disability determinations.

Things to consider:

1. Check with your district to make sure use of any professional is consistent with certification requirements and high-quality teaching parameters set by your district or state.

2. Redirect or reconstitute your "Child Study Team." Call it something else so that people do not associate it with referral to special education. Use this new group to bring together processes that may now be separate (i.e., all struggling students under the same umbrella).

3. Designate an RTI point person as opposed to a special education coordinator at your school.

4. Decide what clerical support versus professional expertise is needed for tasks.

5. Consider new hires in the light of your RTI needs; for example, hiring a teacher who has experience with intervention or hiring a coach to support differentiated instruction.

Facilitating the Change Process

Depending on your starting point, you may be well on your way to having a fully developed RTI initiative or you may have many pieces to put in place. Either way, change is never easy. As an instructional leader, one of your major tasks is to facilitate the change process.

Understanding and Managing Change

The following change facilitation principles are taken from Hall and Hord (2006) and applied to RTI to help put this process in perspective.

- Change is a process, not an event. Declaring "Our school is now doing RTI" will not make it so. As William Bridges (2003) points out, it is important to consider the human side of change, understanding what people go through when they are asked to abandon a comfortable position with the known to venture forth into the unknown. In RTI, teachers and support personnel will have to adapt to new roles and processes, and this will take time. You should expect that full implementation will take 4 or 5 years, requiring patience and perseverance.

- There are significant differences in what is entailed in developing an initiative and implementing it. You would not want to spend a lot of time upfront in the development stages and slack off as your RTI approach is underway. As you implement RTI, professionals will need ongoing support; processes and procedures will need to be refined.

- Administrator leadership is essential to long-term change success. School-level administrators need to be actively engaged in leading the effort and providing necessary resources. Perhaps the biggest challenge is reallocating human resources by helping professionals to redefine their roles.

- Facilitating change is a "team" effort. You might consider creating a process whereby building administrators and a teacher leader group can help set the direction for the initiative, monitor its effectiveness and efficiency, and make recommendations for changes. Engaging families in facilitating change, especially as it relates to their understanding of RTI and involvement with their children, is also an important component.

- Appropriate interventions reduce resistance to change. Hall and Hord (2006) use the term "interventions" to mean actions taken to facilitate change. For example, a building administrator who knows that a teacher is not sold on differentiated instruction may arrange for that teacher to visit another teacher's classroom where differentiated instruction is being used successfully. It would be unrealistic to expect all teachers to love the idea of RTI; some will resist. Taking positive actions to overcome resistance to your adoption of RTI is part of your role.

Obtaining Buy-In From Stakeholders

It is impossible to launch, let alone sustain, a complex initiative without having a commitment from the administrators, teachers, support personnel, and families involved. Therefore, obtaining buy-in from them is crucial to launching an initiative. It is important to realize that buy-in is a process that occurs over time. Upon first hearing about RTI, an individual may think that it makes sense and may be willing to pursue it. However, it is not possible for potential RTI users to buy in to the depth needed for adoption when they have limited information about RTI. It doesn't matter how many times you explain it initially, stakeholders will need absorption time. Further, willingness to adopt RTI becomes more problematic as users have to change practice. Those who thought it was a good idea and seemed to buy in at the beginning may balk when they have to do business differently.

Maintaining Your Focus

As you launch an initiative, you have to be careful to concentrate time, effort, and resources in the direction you are heading. The principle of "Less is more" should be your guide. If you have too many initiatives going on at once, you will dilute your effort. For one thing, human beings can only pay attention to so many things at once. Another issue is that you can minimize the effectiveness of resources by spreading them too thin and ultimately not accomplishing any substantive change. Remember, it takes about 4 or 5 years to have an RTI framework in place. It may take less time if you already have many building blocks in place. You have to be willing to stay the course and help others sustain their efforts.

Designing and Implementing High-Quality Professional Development

Professional development is key to adopting RTI. An initial professional development goal would be to promote shared understanding of RTI on the part of stakeholders. However, as we pointed out when discussing buy-in, understanding does not occur overnight. Work you do in creating shared understanding should be viewed as a recursive process. You will need to cycle back to RTI elements as people get into the process in greater depth. Targets for professional development might include:

- Rationale for RTI and how it relates to what we have been doing (building blocks already in place)

- Our RTI focus and student outcomes, description of our approach and its relationship to our school improvement plan

- High-quality instruction/intervention, differentiated instruction, importance of fidelity of implementation

- Our tiered system, activities within the tiers, collaboration across the tiers

- Data-based decision making using universal screening and progress monitoring, our data management system

- Understanding each others' roles (e.g., general classroom teachers, special education teachers, speech-language pathologist, school psychologist, reading coach)

- Specific professional development around the scientifically based programs or methods you are using throughout the tiers

According to the National Staff Development Council (NSDC) (2001) professional development should be results-driven, standards-based, and job-embedded. The following NSDC standards should guide your development of inservice opportunities in launching your RTI initiative:

Context Standards

Staff development that improves the learning of all students:
- Organizes adults into learning communities whose goals are aligned with those of the school and district.
- Requires skillful school and district leaders who guide continuous instructional improvement.
- Requires resources to support adult learning and collaboration.

Process Standards

Staff development that improves the learning of all students:
- Uses disaggregated student data to determine adult learning priorities, monitor progress, and help sustain continuous improvement.
- Uses multiple sources of information to guide improvement and demonstrate its impact.
- Prepares educators to apply research to decision making.
- Uses learning strategies appropriate to the intended goal.
- Applies knowledge about human learning and change.
- Provides educators with the knowledge and skills to collaborate.

Content Standards

Staff development that improves the learning of all students:
- Prepares educators to understand and appreciate all students; create safe, orderly and supportive learning environments; and hold high expectations for their academic achievement.
- Deepens educators' content knowledge, provides them with research-based instructional strategies to assist students in meeting rigorous academic standards, and prepares them to use various types of classroom assessments appropriately.
- Provides educators with knowledge and skills to involve families and other stakeholders appropriately.

Based on the evidence from professional development research, there is growing recognition among educators that sustained professional development is needed to help teachers implement new practices and processes, and that providing a single workshop will not result in implementation. We also recognize that the task of professional development is to help people grow, and that this process differs from one person to the next in terms of timelines and activities conducive to their learning. Conceptualize professional development in the same way you do core instruction for your students—it needs to be differentiated to meet the needs of adult learners. A challenge you face is to orchestrate a professional development program that meets the learning needs of all professionals at your school to promote use of effective scientifically based instruction/intervention, and data-based decision making that are at the heart of RTI.

Things to consider:

1. By buying a program or a screening instrument you are not "doing RTI." You have merely purchased a tool for implementing the framework. You will need many tools and processes for implementation.

2. In designing supplementary services take care to augment, rather than supplant, instruction. For example, removing a student from fifth-grade language arts instruction in the general classroom so he can receive help with comprehension is supplanting core instruction. That student will be missing work on important fifth-grade language arts standards unless that instruction is provided.

Scenarios

Elementary School

The teacher leadership team at an elementary school who has been working with the principal in launching an RTI initiative comes up with a plan for Tier 2 in which the Title 1 teacher works with small groups of first-graders struggling with math during their regularly scheduled math time with the first-grade teacher. The principal asks them to go back to the drawing board and come up with a plan for the Title 1 teacher to provide "extra" help with math so that they do not miss their core math instruction. He also noted that the first-grade teachers may need more professional development to help them differentiate their core math instruction.

Middle School

A middle school plans an RTI initiative to address the needs of the school, targeted in its school improvement plan. The principal has heard the rumor that many parents of students with learning disabilities are concerned that their children will no longer receive the services they have been receiving in special education. He addresses this issue at the next schoolwide parent meeting. He takes the opportunity to explain RTI, its rationale, and the place of special education services within an RTI approach. He assures parents that the "specially designed instruction" that is required under IDEA 2004 would remain available to students with disabilities.

> <u>High School</u>
> A high school has been working for several years to establish a schoolwide approach to literacy. In this approach, the Wilson Reading System is used for students reading two or more grade levels below in reading. As the building administrators and faculty on the RTI Leadership Team review what they are doing, they wonder if all students who are below grade level in reading need the Wilson program, which focuses on decoding. They decide that they need to have other measures in place to ascertain the reason or reasons a student is below grade level in reading. They realize that they need more options for students, depending on the nature of their reading problems.

Resources

Establishing a Focus

Observation protocols, focus group samples and questions, surveys, questionnaires, and other techniques to help you examine your specific school improvement concerns.	Annenberg Institute for School Reform *Tools for School-Improvement Planning.* Providence, RI: Brown University. http://www.annenberginstitute.org/tools/index.php
Resources to build capacity to engage in long-term systemic change efforts for improving performance of children, youth, and young adults.	Northwest Regional Educational Laboratory *School & District Improvement* http://www.nwrel.org/scpd/about.html
A document that provides research-based guidance offering six key principles for improvement.	Mid-continent Research for Education and Learning (McRel) *Success in Sight: A Comprehensive Approach to School Improvement* http://www.mcrel.org/pdf/schoolimprovementreform/5052_ir_success_in_sight.pdf
An article addressing various RTI approaches	VanDerHeyden, A. (n.d.). *Selecting an RTI model.* RTI Action Network http://www.rtinetwork.org/Learn/What/ar/ApproachesRTI
NJCLD position paper on RTI within the context of learning disabilities, including learning disabilities determination.	National Joint Committee on Learning Disabilities (NJCLD) *Responsiveness to Intervention and Learning Disabilities.* http://www.ldonline.org/article/11498?theme=print

Employing High-Quality Instruction

Databases and user-friendly reports that provide education consumers with high-quality reviews of the effectiveness of replicable educational interventions (programs, products, practices, and policies) that intend to improve student outcomes.	What Works Clearinghouse http://ies.ed.gov/ncee/wwc/
Document explaining the critical elements of an effective reading program in elementary school.	Torgesen, J., Houston, D., Rissman, L., & Kosanovich, K. (2007). *Teaching all students to read in elementary school: A guide for principals.* Portsmouth, NH: RMC Research Corporation, Center on Instruction. http://www.fcrr.org/Interventions/pdf/ Principals%20Guide-Elementary.pdf
A "quick-start" guide for a school-level reading initiative.	Torgesen, J., Houston, D., & Rissman, L. (2007). *Improving literacy instruction in middle and high schools: A guide for principals.* Portsmouth, NH: RMC Research Corporation, Center on Instruction. http://www.fcrr.org/Interventions/pdf/ Principals%20Guide-Secondary.pdf
Book synthesizing research in effective instruction.	Marzano, R. (2003). *What works in schools.* Alexandria, VA: Association for Supervision and Curriculum Development.
Book explaining how school leaders can support the development of differentiated classrooms.	Tomlinson, C. A., & Allan, S. D. (2000). *Leadership for differentiating schools and classrooms.* Alexandria, VA: Association for Supervision and Curriculum Development.
Book explaining how teachers can provide differentiated instruction.	Tomlinson, C. A. (2001). *How to differentiate instruction in mixed-ability classrooms.* (2nd Ed.) Alexandria, VA: Association for Supervision and Curriculum Development.

Building a Tiered System of Instruction/Intervention

Analysis of specific reading programs and data regarding their effectiveness.	Florida Center for Reading Research reports of reading programs http://www.fcrr.org/FCRRReports/CReportsCS. aspx?rep=supp
Free tools and resources to help school staff and parents promote positive classroom behaviors and foster effective learning for all students.	Intervention Central http://www.interventioncentral.org/
Professional development enhancement materials to prepare current and future school personnel to work with students with disabilities in inclusive settings.	The IRIS Center http://iris.peabody.vanderbilt.edu

Creating a System of Data-Based Decision Making

Links to many CBM resources	Curriculum-Based Measurement Warehouse http://www.interventioncentral.org/htmdocs/interventions/ cbmwarehouse.php
Presentations and documents from the Summer Institute on Student Progress Monitoring held by the National Center on Student Progress Monitoring in 2007.	National Center on Student Progress Monitoring http://www.studentprogress.org/
PowerPoint presentation from the 2007 Summer Institute on Student Progress Monitoring explaining the work of the National Center on Student Progress Monitoring and their review of progress monitoring tools.	Short, S., & Went-Yu Lee, S. (2007). *Choosing a progress monitoring tool that works for you.* The National Center on Student Progress Monitoring. www.studentprogress.org/summer_institute/ 2007/tools/ ChoosingaToolPPT_2007.ppt

A learning module to help leadership teams support classroom teachers in developing and effectively using student progress monitoring data to increase achievement.	Deno, S., Lembke, E., & Anderson A. *Progress monitoring: Leadership team activities.* http://www.education.umn.edu/EdPsych/Projects/cbmMODldrshp.pdf
PowerPoint presentation from the 2006 Summer Institute on Student Progress Monitoring providing guidance to administrators	Lembke, E., & Saenz, L. *Supporting teachers who are implementing student progress monitoring: A guide for administrators.* The National Center on Student Progress Monitoring. http://www.centeroninstruction.org/files/PPT_Support.pdf

Developing Infrastructures for Collaboration

This resource is a collection of position papers from many professional organizations, providing information about the roles of various school personnel in RTI.	*New roles in Response to Intervention: Creating success for schools and children* Available on several websites, including: http://centeroninstruction.org/files/rti_role_definitions.pdf
A parent advocacy brief that gives basic information in a user-friendly style.	*A Parent's Guide to Response-To-Intervention* National Center for Learning Disabilities www.LD.org
This book discusses collaboration as it occurs in all of its varying contexts in schools.	Pugach, M., & Johnson, L. (2002). *Collaborative practitioners, collaborative schools* (2nd Ed.). Denver, CO: Love.

Facilitating the Change Process

Book explaining leadership principles that promote broad systems change.	Fullan, M. (2005). *Leadership & sustainability: System thinkers in action.* Thousand Oaks, CA: Corwin Press.
Standards for conducting high quality professional development.	*The National Staff Development Council's Revised Standards for Staff Development (2001)* http://www.nsdc.org/standards/about/index.cfm
Book describing the "nuts and bolts" of instructional coaching. It explains the essential skills that instructional coaches need.	Knight, J. (2007). *Instructional coaching: A partnership approach to improving instruction.* Thousand Oaks, CA: Corwin Press.
A brief article on the use of coaches to support RTI implementation.	Casey, A. (n.d.). *Coaching: A tool for RTI implementation.* RTI Action Network. http://www.rtinetwork.org/Connect/Blog/Coaching-A-Tool-for-RTI-Implementation
Checklist of components for professional development in reading.	*Guidelines for Reviewing a Professional Development Program in Reading* http://www.fcrr.org/FCRRReports/guides/gpdrrp.pdf
Book explaining a widely used evaluation model for professional development in which the bottom line is improved student outcomes.	Guskey, T. (2000). *Evaluating professional development.* Thousand Oaks, CA: Corwin Press.

References

Batsche, G. (n.d.). *Developing a plan.* RTI Action Network. Retrieved May 8, 2008, from http://www.rtinetwork.org/GetStarted/Develop/ar/DevelopingPlan

Bridges, W. (2003). *Managing transitions: Making the most of change* (2nd ed.). Cambridge, MA: Perseus Publishing.

Collaborative Project. (2006). *New roles in Response to Intervention: Creating success for schools and children.* Retrieved April 4, 2007, from http://centeroninstruction.org/files/rti_role_definitions.pdf

Dynamic Indicators of Basic Early Literacy Skills [DIBELS]. (n.d.). Retrieved May 4, 2007 from http://dibels.uoregon.edu/index.php

Fuchs, D., & Fuchs, L. (n.d.). *What is scientifically-based research on progress monitoring.* National Center on Student Progress Monitoring. Retrieved June 4, 2008, from http://www.studentprogress.org/library/What_is_Scientificall_%20Based_Research.pdf

Graner, P., Faggella-Luby, M., & Fritschmann, N. (2005). An overview of Responsiveness to Intervention: What practitioners ought to know. *Topics in Language Disorders, 25*(2), 93-105.

Hall, G. E., & Hord, S. M. (2006). *Implementing change: Patterns, principles, and potholes.* Boston: Pearson.

Jenkins, J. R. (2003, December). *Candidate measures for screening at-risk students.* Paper presented at the NRCLD Responsiveness-to-Intervention Symposium, Kansas City, MO.

Johnson, E., Mellard, D. F., Fuchs, D., & McKnight, M. A. (2006). *Responsiveness to intervention (RTI): How to do it.* Lawrence, KS: National Research Center on Learning Disabilities. Retrieved June 3, 2008, from http://www.nrcld.org/rti_manual/index.html

National Association of School Psychologists (2006). *The role of the school psychologist in the RTI processs.* Bethesda, MD. Retreived May 4, 2007, from http://www.nasponline.org/advocacy/RTIrole_NASP.pdf

National Center on Student Progress Monitoring (n.d.) *Common questions for progress monitoring.* Retrieved May 16, 2008, from http://www.studentprogress.org/progresmon.asp

National Joint Committee on Learning Disabilities (NJCLD) (2005). *Responsiveness to Intervention and learning disabilities.* Retrieved April, 3, 2008, from http://www.ldonline.org/about/partners/njcld

National Staff Development Council (2001). *National Staff Development Council's standards for staff development, revised: Advancing student learning through staff development.* Author.

Reflection

Think about the components that were discussed in this chapter. What questions do you have about them? Reproduce the following pages to write questions and record responses as you find the answers.

I have these questions about:	I found these answers:
Establishing a Focus	
Employing High-Quality Instruction/ Intervention	
Building a Tiered System of Instruction/ Intervention	

Ehren, B. J., Ehren, T. C., & Proly, J. L. (2009). *Response to Intervention: An action guide for school leaders*. Alexandria, VA. Educational Research Service.

I have these questions about:	I found these answers:
Creating a System of Data-Based Decision Making	
Developing Infrastructures to Support Implementation	
Facilitating the Change Process	

Ehren, B. J., Ehren, T. C., & Proly, J. L. (2009). *Response to Intervention: An action guide for school leaders*. Alexandria, VA. Educational Research Service.

May be reproduced.

Chapter 7:

How Might You Proceed?

While it is important for you to know all the components that are included in an RTI framework, it can be daunting to think that you will have to address all the elements at once. Rely on the conventional wisdom that "Rome was not built in a day." It will take time to put into place a comprehensive RTI initiative, depending on how many of the building blocks you already have. Although we have recommended that you use current practices as a springboard, we urge you to heed the National Association of State Directors of Special Education's (NASDSE) admonition: "RTI is a dramatic redesign of general and special education; both need to change and the entire system needs reform if schools are going to make AYP targets and meet the needs of all students. Tweaking will not be sufficient" (2005, p. 1).

Understanding Phases of Adoption

It is helpful to think about phases of adoption to reinforce the notion that launching an RTI initiative is a process, not an event. Adopting any innovation takes time and deliberate effort. As indicated, it will likely take 4 or 5 years to accomplish this goal. The process involves exploration, planning, implementation, and sustained use. In all cases, we are assuming that you will share leadership with other administrators and instructional personnel (teachers and instructional support personnel). We will outline the goals for each phase.

Exploration

In this phase you consider whether your school is ready for an RTI initiative. Goals include:

- Introduce RTI to administrators, teachers, support personnel, and families.
- Consider the context for RTI adoption:
  - district and state RTI policies and frameworks
  - the reasons for your interest in RTI
  - the school improvement plan
  - other competing initiatives
- Gauge interest of the faculty and community in implementing RTI and their ability to commit to implementation (buy-in).
- Reflect on current status with regard to building blocks of RTI (What pieces do you have in place already?).

- Investigate practical factors:
  - the cost of a schoolwide reform effort
  - the multiyear timeline required to create critical systems
- Make a decision to implement a full RTI initiative or to continue to develop building blocks.

Planning

In this phase, you have committed to adopting an RTI approach and you make plans to get started. However, this process is not really linear and you will cycle back to a planning phase after you reach a specific milestone in implementation (e.g., after a year of implementation). Goals include:

- Ensure that all personnel understand RTI basics.
- Involve key stakeholders in establishing the focus for the initiative.
- Make specific connections to state and district policies and initiatives and incorporate them into schoolwide planning activities.
- Review schoolwide achievement data and discipline data; develop a profile of school work and achievement.
- Review the building blocks in place and determine gaps.
- Make decisions about the nature and structure of tiers.
- Develop short-term, mid-range, and long-term plans for RTI adoption; identify required resources to implement tiers; and develop a budget for implementation.
- Create structures to support RTI efforts, including a team that will handle the processes of data analysis and decision making.
- Define roles of professionals within RTI processes.
- Decide how to actively involve parents in the total process.
- Design professional development for targeted groups of administrators and instructional personnel.

Implementation

This is the phase in which you take action to adopt RTI. This phase may take several years and will likely change after you've been in operation for a while. Goals include:

- Allocate resources (time, money, and people) to carry out the plan, including:
  - Universal screenings.
  - Progress monitoring activities.
- Put infrastructures in place to:
  - Promote networking and dialog among teachers.
  - Manage and analyze data.
  - Monitor fidelity of implementation.
  - Review the effectiveness of components and the total process.

- Conduct high-quality professional development
  - to foster deeper understanding of RTI.
  - to implement high quality instruction and intervention.
  - to employ data-based decision making.
- Support teacher leaders in developing their leadership skills.
- Sustain stakeholders' commitment to RTI (buy-in).
- Review progress in achieving adoption goals.
- Make changes in implementation practices that are ineffective.

Sustained Use

This is the phase you might be tempted to skip. That would be a big mistake! In this phase, you pay specific attention to ensuring that all your efforts pay off. You want to see RTI become part of the fabric of your school, independent of your tenure at the school. Although sustained use comes at the end of an adoption process, you should not wait until then to address it. Many of these goals should be addressed during implementation. Goals include:

- Celebrate successes.
- Applaud the efforts of teacher leaders.
- Refine instructional/intervention and data-based decision-making practices.
- Formalize successful processes and procedures (e.g., develop a guidebook).
- Design dissemination vehicles to capture your successes (e.g., school Web site, parent newsletters, community newspapers).
- Encourage teachers and support personnel to share their experiences with others in the district.
- Design a process to induct new teachers in the process.
- Develop a transition plan, if school leadership is changing.

Alignment With the District

Whether or not your district leaves major decisions to you about how you will design and implement your RTI initiative, you will want to be sure your efforts align with the district. For one thing, you want your efforts with RTI to be sustained over time so that if you should happen to leave the school the initiative will be maintained. Louise Waters of the Stupski Foundation, in "Defining a Comprehensive Aligned Instructional System," points out that, "The primary purpose of systems alignment is to ensure that teachers have the necessary supports and empowerment to enable them to make effective instructional decisions for the full range of students they serve" (Waters, 2008, p. 1). It is the principal's responsibility to align district and school support structures. Another important point is that when there is consistency across schools and classrooms, teachers have a shared frame of reference to serve as a basis for professional dialog.

Action Planning

Reminders

Keep these principles in mind that we have discussed throughout Part 2 of this book.

1. See the big picture.
   Know all the key components of an RTI initiative, even though you should judiciously select manageable goals to start.

2. Less is more.
   Don't try to do all aspects of RTI all at once, and don't try to do several major initiatives together.

3. Rome was not built in a day, and there is no quick fix.
   Full RTI adoption takes time.

4. Events change; people transition.
   Attend to the human side of change.

Next Steps

Your immediate next steps will depend on where you are with building blocks and what you think is the best course for your school, given the context. However, there are several actions that you need to take to address the big picture:

- Provide information to faculty and families about RTI.
- Have discussions among stakeholders regarding school improvement needs and their possible connection to an RTI initiative.
- Take steps to promote initial buy-in for an RTI initiative.
- Gauge initial buy-in.
- Assess building blocks (practices and beliefs) already in place.
- Construct a long-range plan to launch an RTI initiative.
- Select a team to lead RTI efforts from across grades/disciplines and include instructional support personnel (e.g., reading specialists, speech-language pathologists, school psychologists).
- Create infrastructures to facilitate collaboration (e.g., time for planning, etc.).
- Identify initial professional development needs to promote shared understanding and continued buy-in.
- Select RTI components that will be your initial focus.
- Decide on the first steps for implementing RTI.

Gathering Baseline Data

As you embark on your RTI initiative, you will want to gather some baseline data which you will track as you move forward. The following information should be included:

- Number of students referred for a special education evaluation
- Number of students receiving a discipline referral
- Percentage of students at each tier of instruction
- Number of weeks that students receive an intervention
- Number of teachers participating in aspects of RTI
- Number of students in special education
- Amount of time from special education referral to eligibility determination
- Amount of time in special education

For your convenience, a data tracking form for this information is provided on page 101 in Part 3 of this book.

Pitfalls and Possibilities

There are going to be missteps along the way of RTI adoption. If you are a human being, dealing with other human beings within complex systems, problems are unavoidable. We will deal with common problems with implementation in-depth in Part 3 of this book. However, we also want to alert you to pitfalls that may occur when launching an RTI initiative.

Pitfalls	Possibilities
Only special education people spearhead RTI. *This is a problem because RTI will then be viewed as a special education initiative. Surely special educators can be valuable contributors, but if they are the only people out front, people will misunderstand RTI.*	RTI leaders include general, compensatory, and special education professionals.
RTI is discussed as "prereferral" (to special education) procedures. *Calling activities in secondary tiers prereferral activities sends the wrong message. Yes, a student who is not responsive to secondary intervention may continue along the process and be considered for special education services, but you don't want that orientation at the outset.*	Referring students to special education is the last thing on anyone's mind in initially addressing student's learning needs (unless there is a good reason to do so).

Support personnel (e.g., speech-language pathologists and school psychologists) are not on anyone's radar screen regarding RTI. *Because speech-language pathologists and school psychologists may serve more than one school it may be easy to forget to include them in RTI processes. Doing so means ignoring valuable resources.*	Support personnel are central players in RTI approaches.
Professionals are given tasks within RTI models that do not make use of their knowledge and skill set. *An "all hands on deck" approach of assigning tasks within RTI processes just so they get done is not advisable. For example having an SLP administering the DIBELS is probably not the best use of her time and expertise. Being a member of the RTI Management Team and helping to analyze DIBELS results from a language perspective is probably a better use of the SLP.*	Professionals make unique contributions based on their knowledge and skill set.

Scenarios

Elementary School

The district has adopted a new elementary-level reading program this year that is scientifically based. Last year they adopted a new science program. The science program adoption did not go well; teachers did not get the professional development they needed to support implementation. The principal of an elementary school wants to be sure that this does not happen with the reading adoption. Regarding her interest in pursuing an RTI initiative, she reasons that instead of introducing RTI this year as a focus, teachers' attention should be on high-quality instruction, including differentiating instruction with the new reading program. The leadership team concurs. The school decides to invest professional development resources to support teachers in implementing the reading program. The principal will work with the reading coach to ensure fidelity of implementation. She will set up networking structures (classroom visits and study groups) within and across grades so that teachers can get ideas from each other and see the big picture of continuity across the program regarding student outcomes. In fact they are working to develop Tier 1 in an RTI context, but the principal was afraid no matter how careful she was in explaining RTI as a framework, it would be perceived as another "thing" to do by the teachers and would distract from their providing high-quality instruction with the new reading program. She also intends to work with teachers on a mechanism to support students who are having difficulty with the new program. However, she won't say "Tier 2" at this point. To her superintendent, the principal explains that she is attending to the building blocks of RTI.

Middle School

A middle school has an energetic, creative educational leader as principal who is working with a group of teacher leaders to develop a site-based professional development cadre. This principal attends conferences and reads professional literature. She is very excited about several initiatives that she thinks hold promise for her school and brings her ideas to the group to discuss. The teachers appreciate her enthusiasm, but they try to convey the perspective that teachers have been inundated with one professional development initiative after another, with no one lasting past an initial workshop. The teachers implore the principal to focus on providing professional development for the RTI initiative that the leadership team has chosen to implement. They would like to go deeper with professional development activities, revolving around ONE major initiative, as opposed to several that superficially "cover" several areas.

High School
A principal of a high school is interested in exploring an RTI initiative at his school. At first he considers asking the Special Education Coordinator at the school to be the front person for the initiative. He reasons that this professional has expertise in the area of effective interventions. After thinking about it, he decides that having the Special Education Coordinator at the helm may send a counterproductive message to the rest of the faculty. They may perceive RTI as a special education initiative and think that they do not really need to be involved. His final decision is to ask the reading coach to lead a team of professionals, including the Special Education Coordinator, school psychologist, speech-language pathologist, and two general education teachers from the School Improvement Team to help him conduct initial exploration.

Resources

The purpose of the *Blueprint* documents is to provide a framework around which implementation of RTI can be built. This school level *Blueprint* outlines the components of a school level strategy to implement RTI districtwide and provide ongoing support to individual sites.	Kurns, S., & Tilly, W. D. (2008). *Response to Intervention blueprints: School building level edition.* Alexandria, VA: The National Association of State Directors of Special Education (NASDSE). http://www.nasdse.org/Portals/0/SCHOOL.pdf
A Web-based source of research-based information and expert guidance on Response to Intervention.	RTI Action Network www.rtinetwork.org

References

Johnson, E., Mellard, D. F., Fuchs, D., & McKnight, M. A. (2006) *Responsiveness to Intervention (RTI): How to do it.* Lawrence, KS: National Research Center on Learning Disabilities. Retrieved June 3, 2008, from http://www.nrcld.org/rti_manual/index.html

National Association of State Directors of Special Education, Inc. (2005). *Response to Intervention: Policy considerations and implementation.* Alexandria, VA: Author.

Waters, L. (2008). *Defining a comprehensive aligned instructional system to ensure powerful teaching and learning for every student in every classroom.* The Stupski Foundation. Retrieved July 2, 2008, from http://www.stupski.org/documents/Defining%20CAIS_01_08.pdf

Reflection

Given your status with practices and beliefs, think about the components around which your initial efforts will be structure. Use the planning tools on the subsequent pages to engage stakeholders in planning the next steps of your RTI initiative.

RTI Planning Tool—Big Picture

What	Who	When	How
Provide information to faculty and families about RTI.			
Have discussions among stakeholders regarding school improvement needs and their possible connection to an RTI initiative.			
Take steps to promote initial buy-in for an RTI initiative.			
Gauge initial buy-in.			
Assess building blocks (practices and beliefs) already in place.			
Construct a long-range plan to launch an RTI initiative.			
Select a team to lead RTI efforts from across grades/disciplines and include instructional support personnel (e.g., reading specialists, speech-language pathologists, school psychologists).			
Create infrastructures to facilitate collaboration (e.g., time for planning, etc.).			
Identify initial professional development needs to promote shared understanding and continued buy-in.			
Select RTI components that will be your initial focus.			
Decide on first steps for implementing RTI. (See RTI Planning Tool - Details)			

Adapted from Johnson et al., 2006. © Student Success Initiates, Inc. Used with permission. May be reproduced.

RTI Planning Tool—Details

	What	Who	When	How
P D	Develop an ongoing, high-quality professional development program to support the components being put in place.			
	Secure or reallocate resources to ensure support for teachers in new learning.			
	Evaluate the effectiveness of professional development by looking at student outcomes.			
S C R E E N I N G	Select and implement a schoolwide academic and behavior screening program that aligns with your curriculum.			
	Determine and secure the resources required to implement universal screening.			
	Administer the screening measure three times a year (e.g., early fall, midterm, and late spring).			
	Create a manageable database to record student information and scores.			
	Organize the screening results (e.g., graphs and tables) to provide intra- and inter-student comparisons.			
	Add screening results to a database so that students' performance can be monitored over time.			
	Specify written steps to follow when further scrutiny is needed for students judged to be at risk.			
C O R E	Select scientifically based core instruction or behavior management practices.			
	Determine and secure the resources required to implement high-quality core instruction.			
	Monitor fidelity of implementation and appropriate dosage of core instruction and behavior practices.			

	What	Who	When	How
P	Select progress-monitoring instruments/procedures that align with core instruction in targeted areas.			
R	Identify a team and process to analyze progress-monitoring results.			
O	Determine and secure the resources required to implement progress monitoring.			
G	Implement a system of data collection and progress monitoring that includes determining both level and growth rate.			
R	Administer the progress-monitoring measure frequently enough to assess a learner's responsiveness. At Tier 1, weekly or twice weekly.			
E	Administer the progress-monitoring measure frequently enough to assess a learner's responsiveness. At Tier 2, two to five times per week.			
S	Organize results to provide a profile of the student's progress within tiers. This could be a graph of test scores supplemented with student work samples.			
S	Monitor results to determine whether a student is responding to the intervention.			
M	Make decisions about reasonable cut scores to determine movement to Tier 2 and beyond.			
O	Monitor results at the classroom level and make decisions about when teachers or instructional programs require more support.			
N	Ensure time is scheduled and process is established for teams to meet and review student needs.			
I	Ensure that staff can analyze data and use them to make instructional decisions.			
T				
O				
R				
I				
N				
G				

Adapted from Johnson et al., 2006. © Student Success Initiates, Inc. Used with permission.
May be reproduced

	What	Who	When	How
SECONDARY INTERVENTION	Select evidence-based interventions and resources to supplement core instruction for students who are struggling.			
	Adopt a system to measure fidelity of implementation of interventions.			
	Decide when to initiate parent involvement.			
	Develop decision rules (including cut scores) to determine which students are at risk and require more intense instructional support.			
	Determine level of intensity of instruction for Tier 2 (how often, how long, size of instructional group).			
	Schedule time for general and special education teachers to collaborate, observe, implement, and evaluate strategies.			
	Develop and implement a process for collaborating with the problem-solving team and monitoring student movement between Tier 1 and Tier 2.			
TERTIARY INTERVENTION	Create and continue the development, individualization, and intensity of interventions to support specific student needs (how often, how long).			
	Develop decision rules (cut scores, exit criteria) for remaining in or moving out of Tier 2 and beyond (responsiveness vs. unresponsiveness).			
	Create and continue the development of resources on evidence-based instructional strategies to support students with disabilities.			
	Include progress-monitoring records from Tier 1 and Tier 2 when making decisions regarding special education evaluation/eligibility.			
	Develop ways to work as a team to deliver a comprehensive program of accommodations, modifications, and remediation for students with disabilities.			

Adapted from Johnson et al., 2006. © Student Success Initiates, Inc. Used with permission.

May be reproduced.

Part 3

Refining an RTI Initiative at Your School

Advance Organizer

You have launched an RTI initiative at your school. Teachers, support staff, and parents are beginning to understand their new roles and responsibilities within a tiered system of effective instruction/interventions; student progress data are used to make instructional decisions, helping to ensure adequate progress for all students. In this section, we will answer the questions:

- How can you make adjustments in your initiative?
- How can you maintain momentum for your initiative?

What does it mean to refine your initiative? In this section, "refinement" means remaining on the course you have planned by making necessary corrections and changes after careful study and by applying persistent effort to keep the initiative going. Refinement means improving collaboration and communication to become more effective and efficient at achieving your objectives. Refinement will help ensure that you can overcome any obstacles you may encounter and maintain energy and interest in your initiative.

Chapter 8:

How Can You Make Adjustments in Your Initiative?

<table>
<tr><td>
▽ **Studying Your Initiative**
▽ **Scenarios**
▽ **Resources**
▽ **References**
▽ **Reflection**
</td></tr>
</table>

In Part 2 of this book you explored your own rationale for implementing RTI, current practices and beliefs at your school, the components to be considered in launching an RTI initiative, and steps to proceed. Although you may be committed to educational reform, you know there will be stumbling blocks. Expected student gains might not materialize immediately, criticism of change could come from several corners, frustration will occur, and daily pressures could distract you. There is no simple solution to handling these inevitable barriers to implementation, but you can work through them. In this section, we will explore a process to study your RTI initiative and target specific areas for discussion, based on possible trouble spots in key components.

Studying Your Initiative

Refinement is a concept embodied in the cycle of plan-do-study-act (PDSA). Known as the Shewhart cycle or the Deming cycle (Deming, 1993), it is the cornerstone of total quality management (TQM). Although TQM in its entirety is not in widespread use in schools, the PDSA cycle can still be a valuable tool to help refine your initiative.

The PDSA cycle illustrated in Figure 8.1 can be related to your school's initiative as follows:

RTI Process	
What are we trying to accomplish?	Student success
How will we know if a change is an improvement?	Student performance gains
What changes can we make that will result in improvement?	Components of RTI initiative
Plan	Long-range implementation plan
	Short-range plans for specific activities (priorities)
Do	Specific activities
Study	Indicators of implementation present
	Results from specific activities
Act	Refine your plan

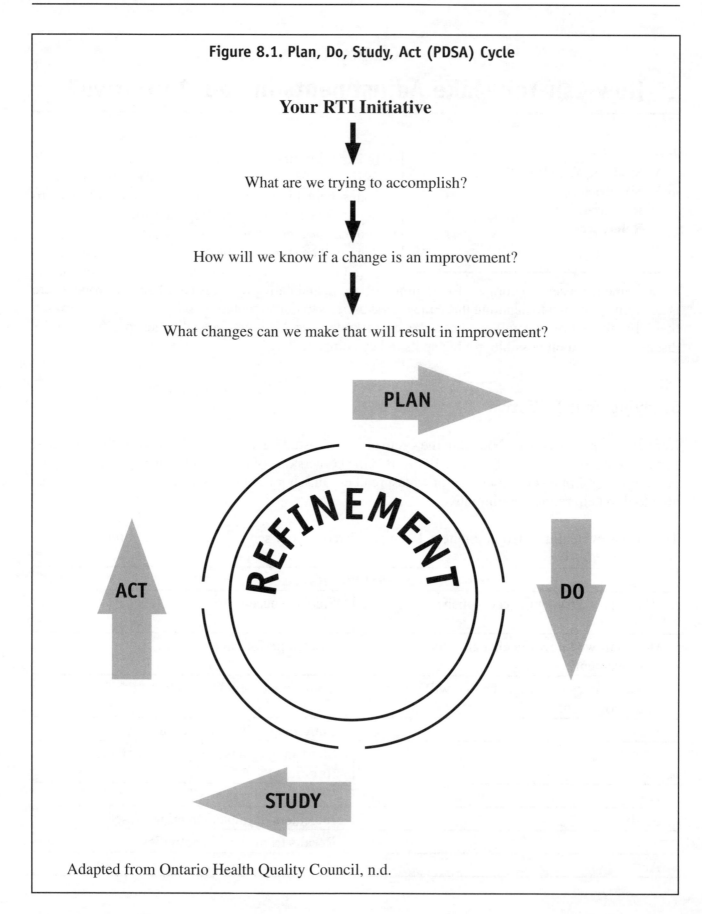

Figure 8.1. Plan, Do, Study, Act (PDSA) Cycle

Your RTI Initiative

What are we trying to accomplish?

How will we know if a change is an improvement?

What changes can we make that will result in improvement?

PLAN

REFINEMENT

ACT

DO

STUDY

Adapted from Ontario Health Quality Council, n.d.

A significant benefit of the PDSA cycle is that it does not require months of planning before implementing aspects of RTI. The school-based leadership team (SBLT) can review the school improvement plan (SIP) to determine the performance areas and performance levels that should be targeted for all students. This team, which typically has broad-based representation from all stakeholders in your school and school community, can evaluate your current beliefs and practices and select priorities for implementation. It is the SBLT that will have the primary responsibility to study what your school is doing to accomplish student success through implementation of an RTI initiative.

The SBLT should consider what method they will use to monitor implementation. The *Colorado Implementation of RTI: A Self-Assessment Tool* (2007) and NASDE blueprints (Kurns & Tilly, 2008), among other documents, can provide a framework that allows the SBLT to determine what changes have occurred at specified points throughout the school year. It is important to make the distinction between having an activity in place as a component of your RTI initiative and studying whether that activity is contributing to your overall accomplishment. This distinction recognizes the reality that the overall gains in student achievement may take time to develop.

The SBLT must also consider a schedule for regular study of the initiative. Since the PDSA cycle can be applied to both short- and long-range plans, the schedules for regular study may vary based on the priority and type of the activity.

Studying the Focus

As you review your initiative the first area of inquiry should be your focus. Are you satisfied that the direction of your initiative is a good fit with the needs of your students and the goals of your school improvement plan? You may have chosen a reading focus initially and now are concerned that your students are having serious problems with writing. If so, you may still focus within the literacy arena, but you will have to widen your scope. You will need to screen and monitor progress in written expression and be sure to identify research-based practices. However, you might have new data that warrants a more drastic change. For example, if your students are experiencing serious problems in math, you may want to include math as an additional focus, without abandoning your existing focus. You may consider a more general problem-solving approach that can address a variety of needs.

Studying High-Quality Instruction/Intervention

As you monitor how well you are doing with primary intervention, secondary intervention, and tertiary intervention, key components of inquiry are: How effective is your professional development program? How efficient is your system of monitoring fidelity of instruction and dosage? How efficiently are you managing time?

Providing High-Quality Professional Development

Effective professional development will be necessary to bring knowledge and skills to your school staff about every aspect of your RTI initiative. Just as the RTI initiative strives to provide what **students** need, professional development must be tailored to what **educators** need. Many professional development opportunities are becoming available in ways that allow "just in time" delivery. Electronic media, the Internet, and portable video/music players allow the dissemination of information without the requirements of travel or face-to-face meetings. Podcasts, streaming video, or DVD self-instructional modules can be accessed at the convenience of the consumer. You, your teachers, and staff may also have available communication systems such as email, video conferencing, and other distance learning opportunities to provide needed support. With these possibilities also come pitfalls. Few of these opportunities extend professional development beyond the awareness stage. They could be helpful as precursors to a total professional development package that includes appropriate demonstration, practice, coaching, and follow-up. They can also be used to orient new staff members to your RTI initiative.

Ensuring the Fidelity of Instruction

As we have noted previously, both NCLB and IDEA require that instruction be based on scientific, research-based practices shown to be effective. Whether in the core curriculum, secondary interventions, or tertiary interventions, including specially designed instruction for students with disabilities, instruction must be delivered with fidelity to the original design principles. Fidelity of instruction involves faithfulness to the scope and sequence of lessons, the protocol of instruction, and the duration and frequency of instruction (also known as "dosage"). One of the greatest dangers to the success of an RTI initiative is a lack of attention to the fidelity of instruction delivery. Without a measure of fidelity, data-based decisions cannot be made. How can you judge how responsive a student is to instruction or intervention if you are not sure how the instruction or intervention is being delivered?

Teachers may have concerns about the RTI initiative because they perceive that it exposes their teaching to much greater scrutiny from the principal and their peers. Teachers need to become comfortable exploring the reasons why a selected instructional or behavioral practice may not be producing the expected results. One way to counter these perceptions is to establish the opportunity for teachers to engage in a self-study of their teaching methods, instructional techniques, and classroom management. Inspection of student performance in individual classrooms should focus first on the core curriculum. Teachers should be trained to study their own delivery of instruction. If your school already supports grade-level curriculum alignment projects and other activities that bring teachers together to improve teaching and learning, then taking on a shared responsibility for student achievement will not be difficult.

Finding the Time

School districts are faced with increasing demands to achieve AYP. Schools are judged based on student performance on state grade-level assessments. Schools can expect that up to 20% of their students might require interventions that are supplementary to the core curriculum or more intense, individual interventions. The challenge for schools is finding time during the day for such interventions. Classroom time is tightly scheduled, often to ensure that students have an uninterrupted block of time for essential instruction, for example, in reading. Transition time is one of the biggest drains on instructional time, whether at elementary, middle, or high school levels. Transition time can take the form of actual travel time from one classroom to another, such as class changes or leaving a classroom for pull-out services. Within classrooms there may be transitions between groups and curriculum areas, such as reading, math, writing, and spelling.

As you study the time required to implement your RTI initiative, it will be important to look for opportunities to use time more efficiently and effectively. Schools could consider using time currently allotted to specials, such as art, music, or physical education. However, state or local requirements may require instructional time in these areas. Since NCLB encourages schools to minimize the removal of students needing such intense instruction, schools might consider after-school programs. Personnel, space, and control issues would need attention with this solution.

Studying the Tiered System

Several questions should be asked about the tiered system: Is our core instruction strong enough? Are professionals assuming productive roles and responsibilities in the process, and are they collaborating in the process? Are we clear where special education fits within the RTI process?

Strength of the Core

Interventions generally take the form of adding more time for explicit teaching of skills to supplement the core curriculum, implementing a supplementary program for specific skill instruction, and providing instruction in small groups or individually. As teachers within grade levels see that there are many students who can benefit from a particular intervention, they may perceive that these interventions are the first defense against school failure. However, Tier 2 interventions cannot resolve problems with the core curriculum. These interventions, while not as time and effort intensive as those at Tier 3, would still drain the school's resources if they are overutilized. Therefore, it is essential to focus on strengthening the core curriculum at Tier 1.

Roles and Responsibilities

An RTI initiative requires that all individuals within a school building have a shared responsibility for student success and school improvement. It may involve assignment of new roles and responsibilities. Classroom teachers have to look to others for assistance and others must be prepared to provide that help. Classroom teachers have traditionally held student success as their primary responsibility. They may have relied upon others, such as guidance counselors, reading specialists, speech-language pathologists, psychologists, educational audiologists, media specialists, specials teachers, and others to provide supplementary instruction, special assessments, or interventions, but may not have thought about the importance of integrating these elements with classroom instruction.

As these other educators begin to take on direct and indirect roles in RTI, integration of services becomes essential. Their direct involvement in the development of an RTI initiative must begin with participation in the planning, analysis, review, and selection of the core curriculum and then extend to deliberations about monitoring progress and decision making about interventions. Their expertise can be very helpful to a team of educators attempting to analyze reasons for a student's difficulty.

Further, the notion that all educators are equally responsible for all the students in their building is a cornerstone of RTI. This requires collaboration, and collaboration is not usually easy. Professionals who are not used to working in tandem need considerable professional development to promote productive partnering. They also need supportive infrastructures to facilitate their working together.

Accommodations, Specially Designed Instruction, or Other Interventions?

At some point, it may seem that a student needs the kind of intense intervention associated with special education. Whether your RTI iteration includes two, three, four, or more tiers there will come a time when the school team must consider a referral for a comprehensive evaluation which should include use of RTI-generated data. Procedural requirements for IDEA direct the school team to pursue a referral if they have information that a student has or may have a disability. If a student is eligible for special education services, then the Individualized Education Program (IEP) will specify the "specially designed instruction" (i.e., special education intervention) and accommodations needed by the student.

While students with disabilities are entitled to reasonable accommodations to help them succeed in school, it is important to recognize that accommodations are not interventions. They are not instructional; they only "level the playing field" for students with disabilities. Accommodations should only be considered after a determination of a disability has been made. However, if a student is at risk, the school can begin interventions immediately in a Tier 2 or Tier 3 context, outside of special education. Occasionally, a student will have an eligible disability under Section 504, not IDEA 2004, and accommodations will be needed in that case.

Studying Data-Based Decision Making

In recent years, a principal's office is likely to be festooned with chart paper indicating performance results from individual classrooms and students. The amount of information, and the ability to collect and analyze it, are all important issues associated with data-based decision making.

An RTI initiative will change the way data is viewed. A major difference is the shift from analyzing student performance as a discrepancy or deviation (usually from some arbitrary expectancy level) to a longitudinal yardstick. Teachers may have difficulty making this shift. Teachers have judged student performance holistically and in a formative manner. Progress data was seen primarily as progress from grade to grade, with intermediate data points at broad intervals at the semester, midterm, and year end.

Gathering and analyzing data longitudinally will mean establishing more frequent benchmarks. Data points create a roadmap to inform teachers if progress is good, questionable, or poor. Good progress would be defined as a student showing expected skill development at a rate that could be expected to close the gap between current levels and the benchmark level. Questionable progress may reflect skill development but insufficient progress towards closing the gap. If neither skill development nor rate of acquisition are evident, responsiveness to instruction/intervention would be poor.

Studying the Infrastructures

An important inquiry about your initiative revolves around the internal structures in place to support the work involved. Do you have sufficient infrastructures and are they working? Look to the logistics of operating the initiative, including the data gathering and management procedures, as well as the team processes for making decisions. Factors include time allocated to essential tasks, budgetary support for systems and materials, scheduling considerations to permit collaboration, mechanisms for delivering high-quality professional development, and shared leadership frameworks. As the expression goes, "The devil is really in the details" and problems in implementation may stem from the lack of specific infrastructures to support the initiative.

Studying the Change Process

Important questions about the change process that target typical problem areas are: How much change is occurring? To what degree are parents a part of the process?

How Much Change?

The bottom line in your change process is the achievement of your targeted outcomes for school improvement. The specific skill areas targeted for change, the rate of change, and the final achievement levels will have to be determined at the school level. A positive outcome would be defined as significant improvement that closes the achievement gap in a timeline established by the team. A questionable outcome would be defined as an improvement, where the rate of closing the gap is less than desired to ultimately achieve the achievement goal in a reasonable time frame. A poor outcome is any condition in which the gap continues to widen. This could occur even if there was measurable improvement.

As a result of screenings and progress monitoring you will have a lot of data. An important consideration is how you will organize these data to know how well you are doing in meeting outcomes. You will also use these data to report outcomes to your stakeholders. An important point is that reports to parents of students who may be at risk should be made at shorter intervals than schools have been accustomed to making.

Parent Involvement

Parent involvement in an RTI initiative at the school is essential—both to the success of individual students as well as the overall school improvement effort. Timely and appropriate parent notification and involvement can prevent problems from occurring. For parents, three important areas are:

1. early identification that their child is at risk for possible problems in school performance;

2. a concise description of problem areas and the interventions that will be attempted; and

3. regular and frequent reports of progress towards specific performance benchmarks, as mentioned above.

If parent information about RTI is important, then parent involvement in the RTI process is essential. Schoolwide screening and frequent assessment of benchmarks will quickly identify a child in need of some additional help. Parents will need information about the purpose of schoolwide screening and what designations of low, moderate, or high risk mean. How teachers and others speak to parents about these concepts can affect a parent's acceptance of change.

Parents will need information explaining how instructional decisions are made for their child. Of particular importance will be issues related to grouping and regrouping of students. Parents may have had experience with ability grouping within prior remedial education alternatives. Interventions within an RTI context differ from these concepts in important ways. First, interventions are not based on ability, *per se*. They are based on skill performance. Second, interventions are designed to close the gap in performance and to do this in a period of time to prevent further decline. Finally, interventions in preliminary tiers are not long-term. They are intended to return students to the core curriculum on grade level.

IDEA provides for specific requirements and procedural safeguards concerning parent notification when the school considers a change in a child's identification, placement, or program. However, assistance within preliminary RTI tiers presents a different scenario. As the school team marshals it's resources to help the student, there may be no need to consider the possibility that the student may have a disability; therefore, because the data are being gathered for instructional purposes, parental consent is not required. However, schools may need to make a decision about requesting consent for a comprehensive evaluation. Because of changes to IDEA in 2004, a parent request for a comprehensive evaluation must be carefully considered. Should parents refuse consent, they will also be waiving their child's right to a free appropriate public education (FAPE). Carefully documenting the results of an intervention may provide the information that is needed for a parent to make an informed choice about consent. Once received, consent affords the parent procedural safeguards, including an evaluation time limit. Nevertheless, intervention activities in preliminary tiers can continue while the evaluation process begins. Informal assessments and information gleaned from these interventions can be used when the school team convenes as an eligibility/IEP committee.

Scenarios

Elementary School
An elementary school had put in place a teacher assistance team responsible for helping teachers support students who were having difficulties in the classroom. The team included a school psychologist, special education teacher, literacy coach, speech-language pathologist, and assistant principal. In reviewing the school's RTI progress, the SBLT studied this process and determined that teachers typically spend 6 to 12 weeks attempting minor changes in instruction before alerting the team that a student is not making sufficient progress. The SBLT wanted teachers to have more immediate and specific support to make effective changes in instruction. They decided to set aside a period of time during grade-level meetings each month to discuss specific students' needs.

Middle School

At a middle school volleyball game, an assistant principal of the host middle school chats with the visiting school's AP about the RTI initiative at the host school, reporting satisfactory progress with the goals that had been established and the plan that had been put in place for implementation. The visiting AP takes notes about the features of the host school's RTI initiative and brings the idea back to her school. The host school generously shares the forms it is using in the process. The visiting school is happy to have concrete ideas that have worked in another middle school. However, the piece they omit is the substantive professional development that has taken place at the other school to pave the way for RTI and help teachers learn specific components of implementation. It is not surprising that at a later volleyball game the once enthusiastic newcomer to RTI is very disappointed with her school's progress to date.

High School

A high school began an RTI initiative this year and is struggling with coordination of the processes needed. Although many of the teachers are not overwhelmingly enthusiastic about working with others on progress monitoring, the practical obstacle is that there is not time built into the school day for the kind of collaboration that has to take place. Creating this infrastructure is at the top of the principal's to-do list. Scheduling common planning time for educators who need to be frequent collaborators is one way he hopes to accomplish this goal.

Resources

Documents related to addressing problem behavior exhibited by students.	Center for Effective Collaboration and Practice. Functional Behavior Assessment. http://cecp.air.org/fba
Workshop video series on functional behavior assessment and intervention planning available for purchase.	Center for Effective Collaboration and Practice (n.d.). *Functional assessment and behavioral intervention plans.* http://cecp.air.org/fba/gablequinn.asp#1
Web site with tools and links to other resources	Florida Problem Solving and Response to Intervention Project. http://floridarti.usf.edu/index.html
Checklist to guide implementation assessment.	Florida Problem Solving and Response to Intervention Project (2007). *Self assessment of problem solving implementation* http://floridarti.usf.edu/resources/presentations/2008/CurtisNASP2008/SystemsChange/SAPSI.pdf

References

Colorado Department of Education (2007). *Implementation of RTI: A self-assessment tool.* Retrieved June 5, 2007, from http://www.cde.state.co.us/cdesped/RTI.asp

Deming, W. E. (1993). *The new economics for industry, government & education.* Cambridge, MA: Massachusetts Institute of Technology Center for Advanced Engineering Study.

Ontario Health Quality Council (n.d.). *Improvement: Testing and implementing change.* Retrieved July 8, 2008, from http://www.ohqc.ca/en/change_2.php

Kurns, S., & Tilly, W. D. (2008). *Response to Intervention blueprints: School building level edition.* Alexandria, VA: The National Association of State Directors of Special Education (NASDSE). Retrieved June, 6, 2007, from http://www.nasdse.org/Portals/0/SCHOOL.pdf

Reflection

1. What is the time frame for regularly studying various RTI components?

   Focus _____

   High-Quality Instruction/Intervention _____

   The Tiered System _____

   Data-Based Decision Making _____

   Infrastructures _____

   The Change Process _____

2. Prior to starting your RTI initiative, we prompted you to capture baseline data in specific areas. Now is the time to consider follow-up data and activities to determine if changes have occurred over time, and possible reasons for the change.

	Baseline	Follow-up	Changes Over Time	Possible Reasons for Change
Number of students referred for a special education evaluation				
Number of students receiving a discipline referral				
Percentage of students at each tier of instruction				
Number of weeks that students receive an intervention				
Number of teachers participating in aspects of RTI				
Number of students in special education				
Amount of time from special education referral to eligibility determination				
Amount of time in special education				

Chapter 9:

How Can You Maintain Momentum for Your Initiative?

▽ **Aspects of Maintaining Momentum**
▽ **Challenges to Sustainability**
▽ **Scenarios**
▽ **Resources**
▽ **References**
▽ **Reflection**

It could be said that the best short-term solution to school improvement is a long-term plan. There is no quick fix, no single program that will solve all the problems. For your initiative to take hold, your school must be into it for the long haul. The good news is that success, even in small increments, leads to greater motivation for further effort. So, while planning is essential, an RTI initiative does not require extensive time in planning before implementation. Maintaining the momentum for your initiative is dependent on employing procedures and activities that will sustain your initiative.

Aspects of Maintaining Momentum

Studying all aspects of your initiative during its implementation and making needed changes will go a long way to maintain your momentum. The PDSA cycle, outlined in the previous section, helps prevent problems from becoming major roadblocks. Your RTI initiative was initially fueled by the realization that the status quo was not acceptable. As you achieve success, you cannot be satisfied that you have merely gone beyond the status quo.

Keeping Stakeholders Interested in the Initiative

An important goal is sustaining everyone's enthusiasm for the initiative. As people become involved in other things, they may become distracted from the focus of your RTI initiative. Also, as the going gets rough, as it may, people's interest may wane as the initiative becomes harder and requires more work to accomplish. Keep it uppermost in stakeholders' minds by engaging in frequent conversations and activities about RTI that relate directly to them.

For example, make sure parents understand that RTI affects their child.

When a parent says:	*You might respond:*
How will I know if my child is participating in RTI?	Every child in our school participates in RTI is some way or another. A key component is high-quality instruction in classrooms. If your child has learning or behavior problems that interfere with his performance in school, he may need more help than his classroom teacher can provide. Our RTI Leadership Team may recommend a Tier 2 intervention for him that would likely be of short duration. However, we would not take any action without involving you in the decision-making process.

Staying on the Same Page

As you implement more components of RTI and your initiative becomes more complex, the danger exists that you may leave some stakeholders behind. They won't all progress in understanding or in action at the same rate. Adhering to timelines, archiving, and requiring compliance around decisions are specific means of staying on the same page.

For example, make sure teachers adhere to agreed-upon decisions.

When the classroom teacher says:	*You might respond:*
I didn't know we were going to have to go to that professional development strand.	Let me go back to the notes of the PLC groups when we decided what kind of professional development we needed in order to implement scientifically based instruction in core classes. I think we agreed that this professional development strand was essential to improve the quality of our instruction. I will verify that and get back with you.

Distributing Credit for Success

"Nothing succeeds like success." In order for your RTI initiative to be successful, individual participants have to meet with success. These personal achievements have to be applauded and advertised consistently.

For example, praise and advertise the efforts of specific participants.

When the school psychologist says:	*You might respond:*
I am concerned that this work with RTI is taking too much of my time.	I really have appreciated your working with us to design our progress monitoring system. I think if you continue to take a proactive role with teachers in helping make the system work, it will decrease the number of special education referrals and you won't spend as much time on that. I have a call in to the Director of Psychological Services to tell her about the major contribution you are making to the success of our RTI initiative at this school.

Exert Leadership Within the District and State

RTI initiatives will require school leaders to advocate for changes in local and state policies and perhaps state law. Changes may be required to remove barriers to implementation, such as class size limits, specific course timeframes, and course code directories that specify teacher certification requirements for teaching in specific areas. Other requirements might need to be established that would provide increased support for RTI actions, such as blended funding from various sources, changes in eligibility criteria for students with disabilities, and school accountability standards.

For example, promote the value of RTI by highlighting your successes to others in your district.

When a principal of another school in your district says:	*You might respond:*
I don't know how we can be expected to implement anything new with no new funding.	Actually, I am finding that RTI is not totally new and is very much in keeping with reforms I have been targeting in my school improvement plan for several years. I did have to rethink the allocation of my existing resources to put a workable system in place. For example, my special education teachers now provide services to students with disabilities in general education classrooms. While they are in the classroom they can deliver interventions to other students. (Plus RTI has cut down on the number of students identified as having disabilities.)

Challenges to Sustainability

Sustaining any initiative over time is a challenge, but it is the bottom line in education reform. It does no good to spend a lot of time in start-up efforts, only to abandon an initiative before it becomes instantiated within the school culture. Deshler and Ehren (2008) have identified 10 challenges to the sustainability of RTI initiatives.

1. A compelling need was not identified to start with; hence, there isn't the will to see things through.

   The need may be there but stakeholders may not be insufficiently aware of it. For example, teachers working with average to above average students may not realize the number of struggling learners at the school, nor their specific achievement levels.

2. Teachers and instructional support personnel do not have the shared belief system upon which RTI is based.

> In Part 2 of this book we discussed the beliefs foundational to RTI. It would be highly unlikely for an entire faculty, especially in a large school, to share all aspects of the belief system upon which RTI is based. However, unless professional development addresses the institution of practices to instill these beliefs, you will not sustain your initiative. It is important to note that working on the behaviors emanating from the beliefs will change the beliefs. Working on changing attitudes, apart from changing behaviors is not productive. For example, instead of dealing with teacher attitudes about the potential of all students to learn, give teachers specific research-based tools for effective instruction. When they see all students learning, their belief system may change.

3. Stakeholders do not have a clear understanding of RTI or may have misconceptions.

> As we have said repeatedly, RTI may look very different from place to place and, in fact, a particular iteration may not have the key components that we have been discussing. As stakeholders read and talk with others, they may become confused with your RTI initiative. The other problem we have addressed is that as implementation proceeds, stakeholders need a greater depth of understanding about the process. It is essential that professional development activities be ongoing to enhance understanding at required levels.

4. RTI is perceived as one more "thing" as opposed to a framework for school reform.

> Teachers can be jaded in their view of educational reform initiatives. They may think of RTI as "one more new thing coming down the pike" and expect that "this too shall pass." They need to see how RTI provides a framework for integrating important student achievement goals and school improvement processes. One of the reasons we have not used the word "model" when referring to RTI initiatives is to avoid the orientation of RTI as a single entity.

5. Teachers and instructional support personnel do not continue to buy in to RTI when they are required to change.

> It is easy to buy in to an initiative when it does not directly affect the way you do business. However, teachers are asked to abandon preferred teaching techniques in favor of those supported by empirical evidence they may be less than enthusiastic about RTI.

6. There is not the type of leadership commitment to see the innovation through difficult times.

> This one is especially for you! As the instructional leader of the school, you will have to find ways to sustain the effort in challenging times; for example, when you sustain reductions in enrollment and, therefore, resources.

7. Sufficient attention was not given to building the necessary infrastructure mechanisms (e.g., putting in place and cultivating leadership teams).

> Sometimes you have to go slow to go fast! Rushing into an RTI initiative without building supports for the effort will lead to failure. As we have noted before, the details of implementation have to receive attention.

8. There is no alignment with the district.

> Your initiative has to be in sync with the district paradigms, policies, and resources. Otherwise, your school may be leading a parade with no other marchers. If you were to leave the school, the initiate has to be entrenched sufficiently in the culture of the district for another principal to be able to pick up where you leave off.

9. Competition exists for scarce resources from other initiatives.

> In Part 2, we used the phrase, "Less is more!" Too many initiatives compete not only for financial resources but also for energy resources of those implementing them. Teachers can only pay attention to so many things at once before they experience overload. For survival of their psyche, they may shut down.

10. A failure to realize that all successful change efforts go through ebbs and flows; ups and downs. There is a tendency to search for the "quick fix" and to abandon initiatives at the first sign of difficulty.

As mightily as you may strive to provide excellent leadership and cultivate your RTI initiative, there are things out of your control that will impact it. You have to be flexible enough to ride the ups and downs without getting so discouraged that you abandon it when the going gets rough (as it very well may)!

Scenarios

Elementary School

In the past, the speech-language pathologist (SLP) at the school has relied on kindergarten screening and teacher referrals to identify students who might need further assessment for possible language disability. Now that the school is involved in universal screening of emergent literacy in kindergarten students, the SLP would like to explore how to dovetail these processes, since she recognizes that language and literacy are two sides of the same coin. The RTI Leadership Team on which the SLP serves has met to discuss this, and they have decided the following: Teachers will preselect students whose performance in classroom literacy tasks is indicative of problems. The SLP will conduct the literacy screening on those students so that she can identify any language problems associated with their emergent literacy performance.

Middle School

A middle school has implemented enhancements to the language arts program, designed to increase reading fluency. The implementation plan provides for a rollout in sixth grade language arts during the upcoming school year. The sixth grade language arts teachers collaborated with the sixth grade mathematics teachers to determine ways for the students to graphically depict their gains in reading fluency. The students will use their own data, such as words-per-minute in reading to construct graphs in math. This activity will provide important opportunities for the students to see their progress and also extend the RTI initiative to other content classes.

High School

A principal of a high school has been very successful in hiring new teachers whose beliefs and practices are consistent with an RTI frame of reference. She shared a few of her interview questions with her colleagues at a meeting of high school principals:

- What methods do you use to help English Language Learners master your content?
- What alternative assignments do you offer students in an effort to uncover what they know and can do?
- How do you organize cooperative learning groups in your classroom?
- Why is it important for content-area teachers to attend to literacy skills and strategies?

Resources

Web casts produced by the California Department of Education	http://www4.scoe.net/rti
Book providing suggestions to support lasting change.	Johnson, D. (2005). *Sustaining change in schools: How to overcome difference and focus on quality.* Alexandria, VA: Association for Supervision and Curriculum Development.

References

Deshler, D. & Ehren, B. (July, 2008). *Implementing RTI at the secondary level.* Preconference Institute of the University of Kansas Center for Research on Learning SIM Conference, Kansas City, KS.

Reflection

Consider the following questions during your study of various activities:

What is the new status quo? Where do we go from here? What are our continuing needs?	
How do we know that change has occurred? How do we explain this change to others?	
How do we get more people involved and participating in our initiative? How do the relationships among individuals need to change?	
Who will be the future leaders of the RTI initiative? How will we maintain and promote our shared belief system?	
When we "know what works," how will we institute procedures to bring others on board? Will there be certain "non-negotiables" for certain procedures and programs?	
Have we looked for examples of changes in behavior that will maintain our initiative? Are others asking about our success?	
Are we giving enough opportunity for practice? Is support readily available?	
Do we consider how other ideas for change will affect our initiative or be incorporated into our initiative?	

Epilogue

The intent of this book is to provide direction for school leaders at elementary, middle, and high schools involved in varying stages of exploring, planning, implementing, or sustaining RTI initiatives. It is meant as a practical guide to making informed decisions about a school's work with RTI. Our goal has been to convey the essential nature of RTI and answer many of the questions school leaders have been asking about it. Most importantly, we want to send the message that RTI is not an add-on to existing school improvement efforts, but rather a framework within which to implement those efforts.

As we have noted, this book is not meant to be an encyclopedia of RTI. We attempted to provide enough specific information to bring the big picture message home without getting lost in too much detail. For further detail, we recommend other resources, which are given within the text.

On one level, this book may be viewed as a quick read by an individual school leader. If that perspective encourages a foray into the content, that is a great first step. However, our hope is that readers do more than read this material quickly. It would be most beneficial as a resource to engage others in dialogue and decision-making processes around RTI. Toward that end, we do hope that readers will become activists who use this guide as a tool for ongoing work with RTI, regardless of their current level of implementation.

Most importantly, we hope that after working with this material school leaders and their constituencies come away with the view that RTI is a worthwhile, doable structure to address school reform and that they discover the building blocks already in place in their schools upon which to base next steps. RTI adoption is not without its problems, as we point out throughout the book—too much too soon; rigid adherence to a system that does not respond easily to changes in student needs; and lack of engagement of educators across general, special, and compensatory education, to name a few. There is also the angst that typically accompanies any change process. As with any substantive school improvement initiative, RTI is not for the faint of heart! However, keeping an eye on the prize of improved student outcomes for all children and adolescents in schools will help school leaders to stay the course.

Index

A

Adequate Yearly Progress (AYP)—18, 21, 22, 36, 75, 94
Adoption—11, 12, 63, 75-79, 81, 111
Alignment—75, 77, 94, 107
Assessment—4, 7, 9, 18, 21, 22, 28, 41, 44, 50, 55, 58, 59, 61, 65, 93-95, 97-99, 108

C

Content Enhancement Routine (CER)—54
Core Instruction—8, 10, 45, 53, 55, 56, 65, 66, 85-87, 95
Curriculum-based measurement (CBM)—59, 61, 69

D

Differentiated instruction—xiv, 9, 11, 31, 39, 42, 45, 48, 55, 61-64, 68
Disability determination—62
Dynamics Indicators of Basic Early Literacy Skills (DIBELS)—59, 71, 80

E

ESEA—18
Evidence-based practice—12, 39, 55

F

Fidelity of implementation—6, 51, 53, 60, 64, 76, 81, 85, 87
Formative assessment—7, 55, 59, 61
Free appropriate public education (FAPE)—19, 98

G

General education—5, 6, 9, 11, 19, 20, 25, 26, 36, 44, 47, 55-57, 82, 105

H

High-quality instruction—6, 25, 51, 53, 55, 64, 68, 73, 81, 93, 101, 103

I

Individualized Education Program (IEP)—20, 21, 27, 61, 96, 98
Individuals with Disabilities Education Act (IDEA)—17, 19, 20, 21, 23, 24, 43, 62, 66, 94, 96, 98
International Reading Association (IRA)—3, 4, 17, 61
Intervention log—53
IQ-achievement discrepancy—17, 20, 21

N

National Association of State Directors of Special Education (NASDSE)—4, 5, 75, 82

National Center for Learning Disabilities (NCLD)—5, 6, 70
National Research Center on Learning Disabilities (NRCLD)—6, 7, 18
No Child Left Behind (NCLB)—11, 17, 18, 19, 21, 36, 39, 41, 43, 94, 95

P

Parental involvement—21
Plan-Do-Study-Act (PDSA)—91-93, 103
Prevention—8-10, 43
Progress monitoring—4-7, 9, 10, 12, 26, 55, 56, 58-62, 64, 69-71, 76, 86, 97, 99, 104
Professional development—xiii, 4, 5, 9, 12, 19-22, 40, 42, 47, 49, 53, 61, 64-66, 69, 71, 76-78, 81, 84, 85, 93-95, 97, 99, 104, 106
Professional learning communities (PLC)—47, 48, 104

S

School-based leadership team (SBLT)—93, 98
School improvement —ix, 11, 35, 41, 42, 45, 52, 64, 66, 67, 75, 78, 82, 84, 93, 95, 97, 103, 105, 106, 111
School reform—ix, 29, 46, 67, 106, 111
Scientifically based methods—40, 46, 49
Screening—4-8, 13, 25, 28, 55, 58-60, 62, 64, 66, 72, 76, 85, 97, 108
Sound instruction—39, 40, 45, 47, 49
Special education—3-6, 8-13, 17, 18, 26, 27, 35-37, 40-42, 44-46, 52, 55-58, 61, 62, 64, 66, 75, 79, 82, 87, 95, 96, 101, 104, 105
Speech-language pathologist (SLP)—xiv, 12, 22, 27, 28, 48, 60, 61, 64, 78, 80, 82, 84, 95, 98, 108
Standard treatment protocol—26, 27, 56, 58
Standards—3, 18, 20-22, 36, 37, 40-42, 45-47, 52, 54, 56, 59, 64-66, 71
Student outcome measures—7
Student outcomes—10, 42, 44, 51, 52, 58, 61, 64, 71, 81, 85, 111

T

Tier—ix, 5-7, 9, 10, 12, 25-27, 51, 55-60, 62, 64, 66, 69, 73, 76, 79, 81, 89, 95, 96, 98, 101, 103
Total quality management (TQM)—91

U

Universal screening—5, 7, 13, 58-60, 64, 76, 85, 108

W

Walk-through—40, 53, 54

ERS ORDER FORM FOR RELATED RESOURCES

Quantity	Item Number	Title	Price per Item			Total Price
			Base Price	ERS Individual Subscriber Discount Price	ERS School District Subscriber Discount Price	
	0754	*The School Leader's Guide to Special Education, Second Edition*	$27.95	$19.95	$19.95	
single copy only	5411	*ERS Info-File® Response to Intervention*	$40	$30	$20	
	0538	*Handbook of Research on Improving Student Achievement, Third Edition*	$44	$33	$22	
		Shipping and Handling** (Add the greater of $4.50 or 10% of purchase price.)				
		Express Delivery** (Add $20 for second-business-day service.)				
	**Please double for international orders.				TOTAL PRICE:	

SATISFACTION GUARANTEED! If you are not satisfied with an ERS resource, return it in its original condition within 30 days of receipt and we will give you a full refund.

Visit us online at www.ers.org for a complete listing of resources!

Method of payment:

☐ Check enclosed (payable to ERS)   ☐ P.O. enclosed (Purchase order #_____)

☐ MasterCard   ☐ VISA   ☐ American Express

Name on Card: _____   Credit Card #:_____

Expiration Date: _____   Signature: _____

Ship to: (please print or type)   ☐ Dr.   ☐ Mr.   ☐ Mrs.   ☐ Ms.

Name: _____   Position: _____

School District or Agency: _____   ERS Subscriber ID#: _____

Street Address: _____

City, State, Zip: _____

Telephone: _____   Fax: _____

Email: _____

Return completed order form to:
Educational Research Service • 1001 North Fairfax Street, Suite 500 • Alexandria, VA 22314-1587
Phone: 703-243-2100 • Toll Free Phone: 800-791-9308 • Fax: 703-243-1985 • Toll Free Fax: 800-791-9309
Email: ers@ers.org • Web site: www.ers.org

Experience the ERS Advantage

Save Money. Save Time. Make Better Decisions.

Subscription at a Glance

If you are looking for reliable preK-12 research to . . .

- tackle the challenges of NCLB;
- identify research-based teaching practices;
- make educationally sound and cost-effective decisions; and most importantly
- improve student achievement . . .

then look no further than an ERS Subscription.

Simply pick the subscription option that best meets your needs:

- ■ **School District Subscription**—a special research and information subscription that provides education leaders with timely research on priority issues in preK-12 education. All new ERS publications and periodicals, access to customized information services through the ERS special library, and 50% discounts on additional ERS resources are included in this subscription for one annual fee. This subscription also provides the entire administrative staff "instant" online, searchable access to the wide variety of ERS resources. You'll gain access to the ERS electronic library of more than 1,600 educational research-based documents, as well as additional content uploaded throughout the year.

- ■ **Individual Subscription**—designed primarily for school administrators, staff, and school board members who want to receive a personal copy of new ERS studies, reports, and/or periodicals published and special discounts on other resources purchased.

- ■ **Other Education Agency Subscription**—available for state associations, libraries, departments of education, service centers, and other organizations needing access to quality research and information resources and services.

Your ERS Subscription benefits begin as soon as your order is received and continue for 12 months. For more detailed subscription information and pricing, contact ERS toll free at 800-791-9308, by email at ers@ers.org, or visit us online at www.ers.org!

We want to be your research partner!

Notes

Notes

Notes

Notes